ReadingHorizons®

Student *Workbook*

ReadingHorizons®

Student **Workbook**

Authors:
Heidi Hyte
Shantell Berrett

Contributor:
Alisha Thomas
Michelle Weaver

Cover and Interior Design:
Kedrick Ridges

Student Workbook, Second Edition

Published by
Reading Horizons
60 North Cutler Drive, Suite 101
North Salt Lake, UT 84054
800-333-0054

Printed in the United States of America

Copyright May 2013 by Reading Horizons

No part of this publication may be reproduced, stored in a retrieval system, or transmitted in any form or by any means, electronic, mechanical, photocopying, recording, or otherwise, without the prior permission of the Copyright owner.

ISBN 978-1-62382-084-8

Photo Credits: All photos from ClipArt.com and from Stocklib.com.

Student **Workbook**

Table of Contents

Chapter 1 .... **1-38**
    Lesson 1: Voiced and Voiceless 1-2
    Lesson 2: Letter Group 1 3-4
    Lesson 3: Building Words 5-6
    Lesson 4: Nonsense Words 7-8
    Lesson 5: Letter Group 2 9-10
    Most Common Words List 1 11-12
    Lesson 6: Sentences and Intonation 13-14
    Lesson 7: Letter Group 3 15-16
    Lesson 8: Commas 17-18
    Most Common Words List 2 19-20
    Lesson 9: Letter Group 4 21-22
    Lesson 10: Letter Group 5 23-24
    Most Common Words List 3 25-26
    Lesson 11: Spelling with *C* and *K* 27-28
    Lesson 12: Direct and Indirect Quotations 29-30
    Most Common Words List 4 31-32
    Lesson 13: Alphabetical Order 33-34
    Lesson 14: Articles 35-36
    Chapter 1 Reading in Context 37-38

Chapter 2 .... **39-60**
    Lesson 15: *L*-Blends 39-40
    Lesson 16: Double *S*, *F*, and *Z* 41-42
    Lesson 17: Special Vowel Combinations: *-LL, -NG, -NK* 43-44
    Most Common Words List 5 45-46
    Lesson 18: *R*-Blends 47-48
    Lesson 19: Plurals 49-50
    Lesson 20: Possessives 51-52
    Lesson 21: *S*-Blends 53-54
    Lesson 22: Two Extra Blends 55-56
    Most Common Words List 6 57-58
    Chapter 2 Reading in Context 59-60

Chapter 3 .... **61-94**
    Lesson 23: Short and Long Vowels 61-62
    Lesson 24: Phonetic Skill 1 63-64
    Lesson 25: Phonetic Skill 2 65-66
    Lesson 26: Vowel Families *O* and *I* 67-68
    Lesson 27: Parts of Speech 69-70
    Lesson 28: Adding Suffixes to Phonetic Skills 1 and 2 71-72
    Lesson 29: Three Sounds of *-ED* 73-74
    Most Common Words List 7 75-76
    Lesson 30: Phonetic Skill 3 77-78

Table of Contents

Lesson 31: Phonetic Skill 4 79-80
Lesson 32: Another Sound for *C* and *G* 81-82
Lesson 33: Adding Suffixes to Phonetic Skills 3 and 4 83-84
Lesson 34: Sounds of *GH*, *IGH*, and *IGHT* 85-86
Lesson 35: Phonetic Skill 5 and Adjacent Vowels 87-88
Lesson 36: Adding Suffixes to Phonetic Skill 5 89-90
Most Common Words List 8 91-92
Chapter 3 Reading in Context 93-94

Chapter 4 .... **95-118**

Lesson 37: Contractions 95-96
Lesson 38: Many Jobs of *Y* 97-98
Lesson 39: Decoding Skill 1 99-100
Lesson 40: Syllable Stress and the Schwa 101-102
Lesson 41: Last Job of *Y* 103-104
Lesson 42: Decoding Skill 2 105-106
Lesson 43: Prefixes 107-108
Lesson 44: *-LE* at the End of a Word 109-110
Lesson 45: Decode Words of Any Length 111-112
Lesson 46: Compound Words 113-114
Most Common Words List 9 115-116
Chapter 4 Reading in Context 117-118

Chapter 5 .... **119-172**

Lesson 47: Murmur Diphthong *AR* 119-122
Lesson 48: Murmur Diphthong *OR* 123-124
Lesson 49: Murmur Diphthongs *ER*, *UR*, and *IR* 125-128
Lesson 50: Exceptions to Murmur Diphthongs 129-132
Most Commmon Words List 10 133-134
Lesson 51: Digraphs *CH*, *SH*, *WH*, *TH*, and *TH* 135-138
Lesson 52: More Digraphs *PH*, *GN*, *KN*, *CK*, and *WR* 139-142
Lesson 53: Digraph Blends 143-144
Lesson 54: Digraph Words with Plural Endings 145-146
Most Commmon Words List 11 147-148
Lesson 55: Special Vowel Sounds *AU/AW*, *OU/OW*, *OI/OY* 149-152
Lesson 56: Special Vowel Sounds *OO* and *OO* 153-156
Lesson 57: More Special Vowel Sound Skills 157-158
Most Commmon Words List 12 159-162
Lesson 58: Other Suffixes 163-166
Lesson 59: Adding Suffixes to Words Ending in *Y* 167-168
Lesson 60: Practicing Multi-Syllabic Words 169-170
Chapter 5 Reading in Context 171-172

Student **Workbook**

Table of Contents

Chapter 6 .... **173-192**
    Lesson 61: Decoding Exceptions 173-174
    Lesson 62: Double Consonants and *-KE*, *-CK*, *-K*, and *-C* 175-176
    Most Commmon Words List 13 177-178
    Lesson 63: Letter Combinations that Split 179-180
    Lesson 64: Spelling with *-SS*, *-CE*, or *-SE* 181-182
    Lesson 65: Sounds of *EU* and *EW* 183-184
    Lesson 66: Vowels that Reverse 185-186
    Lesson 67: Other Sounds of *EA* and *IE* 187-188
    Lesson 68: Synonyms, Antonyms, and More 189-190
    Chapter 6 Reading in Context 191-192

Appendix

Posters and Charts **193-196**
Letter Formations **197-200**
Answer Key **201-228**
Glossary **229-230**

Student **Workbook** Name

Lesson 1

Voiced and Voiceless

Skills Review

Voiced (〰)
- Vocal cords vibrate in the throat, causing a vibration.
- Put your fingers on your throat to feel the vibration.
- Voiced consonants are: *b, d, g, j, l, m, n, r, v, w, x* (at the beginning or in the middle of a word), *y, z*.
- All vowels are voiced: *a, e, o, u, i*.

Voiceless (⊖)
- Vocal cords do not vibrate as air passes through them.
- There is no vibration felt in the throat.
- Voiceless consonants are: *c, f, h, k, p, s, t, x* (at the end of a word).

APPLICATION ACTIVITIES

A. Say these pairs of sounds. Put your fingers on your throat. Is the sound voiced or voiceless? (Letters between slashes "/ /" represent sounds.)

1. /b/ (as in boy)   /p/ (as in pan)

2. /f/ (as in fan)   /v/ (as in van)

3. /g/ (as in girl)   /c/ (as in cat)

Lesson 1 Name Student **Workbook**

Voiced and Voiceless

4. /d/ (as in dog)  /t/ (as in ten) **10**

5. /s/ (as in sun)  /z/ (as in zip)

B. Say these sounds again. Write the letter under the 〰 column if the sound is voiced. Write the letter under the ⊖ column if the sound is voiceless.

~~b~~   d   f   g   k
p   s   t   v   z

〰 (Voiced)	⊖ (Voiceless)
b	

ReadingHorizons®

Student **Workbook**   Name

Lesson 2

Letter Group 1

Skills Review

Vowel *A* 👄, Consonants *B* 👄, *F* 😐, *D* 👄, *G* 👄, The Slide
- Vowel *A/a*, as in *at*: sound and letter formation.
- Consonant *B/b*: sound and letter formation.
- The Slide: sliding *b-a* sounds together (ba, /ba/) to help with fluency.
- Consonants *F/f*, *D/d*, *G/g*: sound and letter formation, and slides fa, da, ga.

DECODING

Mark the slide with an arrow underneath.

ba→   fa→

A. Mark and say these slides.

ba→   da   fa   ga

APPLICATION ACTIVITIES

A. Match the uppercase (capital) letter with the lowercase letter.

1. F — b
2. B — d
3. G — f
4. D — g
5. A — a

B. Circle the lowercase letters.

F (b) a G D g B f A d

C. Circle the uppercase (capital) letters.

(B) g A D b F d G f a

Lesson 2 Name *Student* **Workbook**

Letter Group 1

D. Match the correct letter with the picture that begins with that letter.

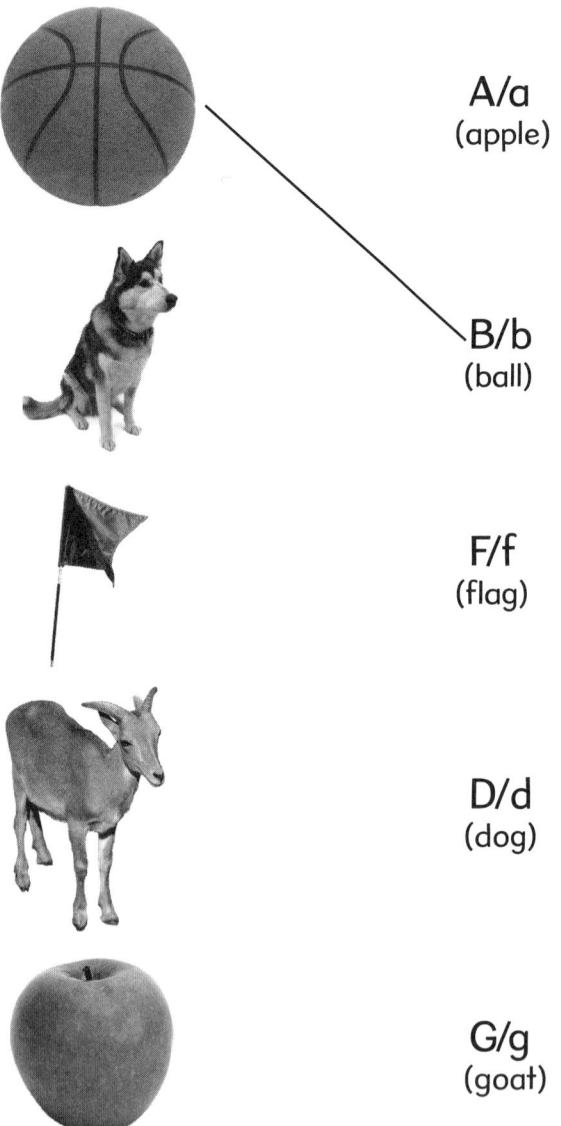

A/a
(apple)

B/b
(ball)

F/f
(flag)

D/d
(dog)

G/g
(goat)

E. (Circle) the letter combinations that are slides.

(ba)   af   da   ag   ga

To practice writing the letters in Letter Group 1, go to page 197.

Student **Workbook**   Name

Lesson 3

Building Words

Skills Review
- Most words have three parts: a beginning, a middle, and an end.
- When a word is formed, drop the slide arrow and slide the sounds together to make a word.
- Identify the vowel in the word by marking an *x* underneath it.

DECODING

Mark the vowels with an *x* underneath.

b*a*g
 x

A. Mark the vowel with an *x*.

b*a*d   gag   fad   gab   dad
 x

APPLICATION ACTIVITIES

A. Choose the correct ending letter to make a real word. Use the picture as a clue.

Example: __gab__ (d/b)

1. ba___ (g/f)

2. ba___ (b/d)

3. da___ (d/f)

Building Words

B. Circle the beginning sound of the word. Put an *x* under the vowel. Put a box around the final sound in the word.

Example: (f)a[b]

b a g   d a b   g a d   g a g

C. Circle the word that rhymes. Remember that words rhyme if the vowel and the ending sound are the same.

Example: bad: (fad) bag

1. **bag:**   gag   gab

2. **dad:**   bad   gab

3. **gab:**   fad   dab

Student **Workbook**   Name

Nonsense Words

Lesson 4

Skills Review
- Nonsense words do not have meanings.
- Nonsense words help with letter/sound knowledge.

DECODING

To mark nonsense words:
1. Mark the nonsense words with an asterisk (*) at the beginning of the word.
2. Mark the vowels with an *x* underneath.

*dag   *faf

A. Draw an asterisk (*) before the word. Then mark the vowel with an *x*.
   Example: *dag

baf   gaf   daf   bab

APPLICATION ACTIVITIES

A. Circle the nonsense words.

bad   *daf   dad   fad   *bab

*dag   *gaf   *faf   *baf   fab

B. Unscramble the letters to make a nonsense word. Remember that the vowel will be in the middle. Use the words in the box as clues.
   Example: *adg *dag*

| *faf   *baf   *bab   *daf |

1. *dfa _____

2. *abb _____

3. *ffa _____

4. *bfa _____

ReadingHorizons®

Student **Workbook**   Name

Lesson 5

Letter Group 2

Skills Review

Consonants H ⊖, J ⌢, L ⌢, M ⌢, Vowel E ⌢
- Consonants *H/h*, *J/j*, *L/l*, *M/m*: sound and letter formation.
- Vowel *E/e*, as in *Ed*: sound and letter formation.
- Make slides and build words using the vowels *a* and *e* with consonant letters in Letter Groups 1–2.
- Mark the vowel in each word with an *x*.
- These are example slides: he→ ja→ le→ ma→

DECODING

Slides
Mark the slide with an arrow underneath.

je→   le→

Words
Put an *x* under the vowel in a word.

bed   leg
 x   x

A. Mark and say these slides.

he→   be   ja   fe   je   la

de   ma   le   me   ha   da

B. Mark the vowel with an *x*.

Meg   jab   led   bad   *heb   *jaf
 x

APPLICATION ACTIVITIES

A. Circle the lowercase letters.

H   M   ⓙ   L   E   h   m   J   l   e

B. Circle the uppercase (capital) letters.

Ⓔ   h   M   e   J   L   m   j   H   l

Lesson 5 — Name — Student **Workbook**

Letter Group 2

C. Match the uppercase (capital) letter with the lowercase letter.

1. H   j
2. J   e
3. L   m
4. M   l
5. E   h

(1. H — h; 5. E — j matched as drawn)

D. Match the correct letter with the picture that begins with that letter.

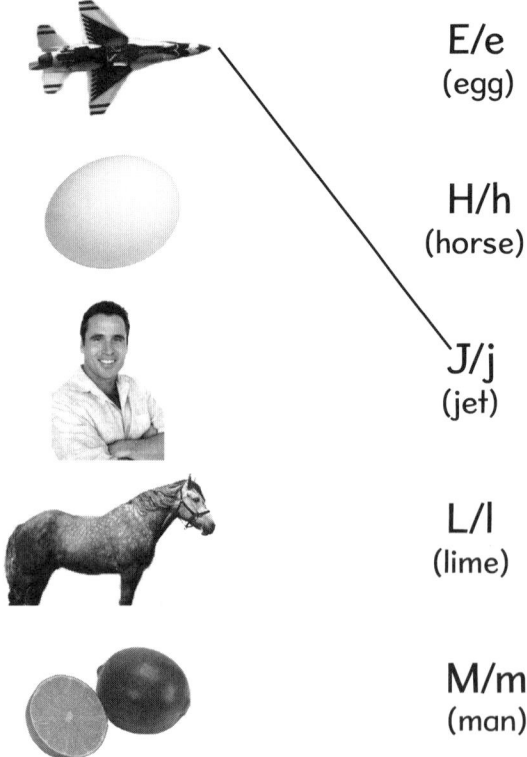

E/e
(egg)

H/h
(horse)

J/j
(jet)

L/l
(lime)

M/m
(man)

To practice writing the letters in Letter Group 2, go to page 197.

Student **Workbook**   Name

MCW 1

Most Common Words List 1

Skills Review
- Most Common Words are words that are used often when reading and sometimes do not follow phonetic skills.

Most Common Words List 1

| the | to | a | and | in | you | that |
| of | it | not | for | I | is | an |

A. Write the missing letters to complete the Most Common Words.

1. t __ e
2. __ h __ t
3. a __
4. __
5. f __ r
6. __ n
7. __ t
8. __ f
9. t __
10. __ s
11. y __ u
12. __
13. __ o t
14. a __ d

B. Read the story. Circle the Most Common Words from List 1.

I set an egg and a ham in the pan. It is too hot. I go to the den.

My dog Jed and my cat Meg get on top of the table.

I go back in the kitchen.

"That ham is not for you, Jed and Meg!"

I *had* an egg and a ham.

ReadingHorizons® 11

Most Common Words List 1

C. One of the words in each set is a Most Common Word, and the other is a nonsense word. Circle the Most Common Word.

Example: (to)   ot

1. of   fo
2. not   tno
3. sa   is
4. that   taht
5. ta   to
6. eth   the
7. an   na
8. Ih   I
9. ib   it
10. for   ofr
11. a   ta
12. yuo   you
13. and   nda
14. ni   in

D. Choose the Most Common Words to complete the sentences.

1. I set _____a._____ egg _____b._____ a ham in the pan. (and/an/is)

2. _____ is too hot. (For/It)

3. I go _____ the den. (an/to)

4. My dog Jed and my cat Meg get on top _____a._____ _____b._____ table. (of/the/is)

5. I go back _____ the kitchen. (in/not)

6. "_____a._____ ham is not _____b._____ you, Jed and Meg!" (of/That/for)

7. _____a._____ had an egg and _____b._____ ham. (a/to/I)

8. It _____ too hot. (is/for)

9. "That ham is _____a._____ for _____b._____, Jed and Meg!" (of/you/not)

Student **Workbook**   Name

Lesson 6

Sentences and Intonation

Skills Review

Sentence Structure
- A sentence is a complete thought.
- Sentences have two parts: a subject and a predicate.
- Every sentence begins with an uppercase (capital) letter and ends with a punctuation mark.

Punctuation
- Sentences that are statements or commands end with a period (.).
- Sentences that ask questions end with a question mark (?).
- Sentences that show excitement or strong feelings end with an exclamation mark (!).

Intonation
- Intonation is the sound and melody of the voice when reading aloud.
- Falling intonation is used with *wh-* questions, commands, and statements.
- Rising intonation is used with yes/no questions and when asking for clarification.

APPLICATION ACTIVITIES

A. Read the sentences. If it is a complete thought, write *S* for "sentence." If it is an incomplete thought, write *P* for "phrase."

   Example: **is in the bed** ___P___

   1. That is not for you. ___

   2. not for you ___

   3. you and I ___

   4. The dog is in the bed. ___

   5. I am sad. ___

   6. The bag ___

B. Write the correct punctuation mark at the end of each sentence. Write a period (.), question mark (?), or exclamation mark (!). Use the facial expressions as clues.

   Example: **Is that you?**

   1. It is you

Lesson 6 — Sentences and Intonation

2. The egg is not bad

3. Stop

4. Is it big

C. Read each sentence. What is the intonation of each sentence? If it ends in rising intonation, draw a line going up (___/) to show rising intonation. If it ends in falling intonation, draw a line going down (‾\ ) to show falling intonation.

Example a: I fed the dog.   Example b: Is that you?

1. Jed is in the den.

2. That is an egg.

3. Is it his leg?

4. I had jam.

5. Is Meg in bed?

6. Is that for Jed and Meg?

Student Workbook   Name   Lesson 7

Letter Group 3

Skills Review
Consonants N ⌒, P ⌢, R ⌒, S ⌢, Vowel O ⌒
- Consonants N/n, P/p, R/r, S/s: sound and letter formation.
- Vowel O/o, as in *on*: sound and letter formation.
- Make slides and build words using the vowels *a*, *e*, and *o* with consonant letters in Letter Groups 1–3.
- Mark the vowel in each word with an *x*.
- These are example slides: no → po → ro → so →

DECODING

Slides
Mark the slide with an arrow underneath.

po→   ro→

Words
Put an *x* under the vowel in a word.

pop   rod
 x   x

A. Mark these slides. Then say them.

ro→   pe   jo   so   lo   ne

se   ra   no   po   he   fe

B. Mark the vowels with an *x*.

mop   red   not   man   *leb   *hod
 x

APPLICATION ACTIVITIES

A. Match the uppercase (capital) letter with the lowercase letter.

N   P   R   S   O

r   n   o   p   s

Lesson 7   Name   Student **Workbook**

Letter Group 3

B. (Circle) the lowercase letters.

R (s) O p N r S o n P

C. (Circle) the uppercase (capital) letters.

(O) p R s o P n N r S

D. Match the correct letter with the picture that begins with that letter.

N/n   P/p   R/r   S/s   O/o
(nest)   (pan)   (road)   (socks) (octagon)

E. (Circle) the letter that could be added to make a real word. Use the picture as a clue. Then write the real word, and mark the vowel with an *x*.

1. pa__      (n) f g   Word: _pan_
                                                    x

2. be__   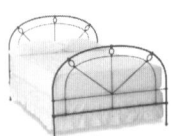   m d b   Word:_____

3. mo__      n j p   Word:_____

4. ne__    g t p   Word:_____

5. ma__    d b n   Word:_____

To practice writing the letters in Letter Group 3, go to page 198.

Commas

Skills Review
- A comma is a punctuation mark that is used to represent a breath or a pause in our reading.
- Commas are used for several different purposes.

Rules for Using Commas

Use a comma to separate two sentences joined with "and," "but," or "or."
>Jan is sad, but Ned is not.
>You can have an egg, or you can have ham.

A comma is used between three or more subjects or when listing words in a sentence.
>Jed, Meg, and Dan are in the van.
>Get me some mops, mats, and rags.

A comma is used in a series between three or more predicates.
>The cat ran to me, rubbed my leg, and had a nap in my lap.
>Deb got the mop, got some rags, and put them in the van.

A comma is used to separate "yes" and "no."
>Yes, I have eggs.
>No, no, no! This pan is hot!

Commas are used to offset names.
>Jan, is this your bag?
>Can you get some nuts, Tom?

Commas separate the name of the day from the date and the date from the year.
>Dad was born May 1, 1951, at 1 p.m.
>Mom was born Sunday, May 11, 1950.

Commas are used to separate the name of a city and a state and after the name of a state when it appears with the city name in the middle of a sentence.
>He drove from Ogden, Utah, to New York.
>Mr. Jones was born in Las Vegas, Nevada.

APPLICATION ACTIVITIES

A. Read the sentences. Add commas where needed.
>Example: **Eggs ham and jam are in the bag.**
>**Eggs, ham, and jam are in the bag.**

1. No the ham is in the bag.

2. Jed met Meg on May 8 1975 in California.

Commas

3. Is dad in the van or is he with Jan?

4. Do you have a ham in your bag Meg?

5. Dad got an egg put it in a hot pan and sat on the bed.

6. Meg has a job in Sacramento California.

7. Don fed his hens pups cats and pigs.

8. Dad Meg and Jed are in the lab.

Student **Workbook** Name

MCW 2

Most Common Words List 2

Skills Review

- Most Common Words are words that are used often when reading and sometimes do not follow phonetic skills.

Most Common Words List 2

on	with	he	at	are	be	this
but	have	we	as	they	will	her

A. Unscramble the letters to form a Most Common Word.

Example: thiw   _with_

1. yhet _____
2. ehav _____
3. thsi _____
4. eh _____
5. reh _____
6. liwl _____
7. ew _____

8. rea _____
9. no _____
10. ta _____
11. thwi _____
12. eb _____
13. sa _____
14. tbu _____

B. Read the story. Circle the Most Common Words from List 2. Words can be used more than once.

This is my family. We are at the park.

This is my mom and dad. They have two kids—my brother and me. The man with the red hat on is my dad. He is tall, but my mom is short.

This is my mom. Her hat is pink.

This is my brother. He is only ten, but he is as tall as my mom! He will be tall like my dad when he grows up.

ReadingHorizons®

Most Common Words List 2

C. Circle the Most Common Word to complete each sentence. Then write the word on the line.
Example: I _have_ a hat. (have/be)

1. _____ is my family. (We/This)

2. We _____ at the park. (are/with)

3. _____ have two kids. (They/Her)

4. The man _____ the red hat is my dad. (that/with)

5. _____ is tall. (He/Her)

6. _____ hat is pink. (Her/We)

7. They _____ two kids. (on/have)

8. _____ are at the park. (As/We)

9. He _____ be tall like my dad. (will/but)

10. My dad is tall, _____ my mom is short. (but/on)

11. The man with the red hat _____ is my dad. (they/on)

12. We are _____ the park. (this/at)

13. He will _____ tall like my dad. (as/be)

14. He is _____ tall as my mom! (as/her)

Student Workbook

Name _____

Lesson 9

Letter Group 4

Skills Review
Consonants T ⊖, V ⌢, W ⌢, X ⊖, Y ⌢, Vowel U ⌢
- Consonants T/t, V/v, W/w, X/x, Y/y: sound and letter formation.
- Vowel U/u, as in *up*: sound and letter formation.
- Make slides and build words using the vowels *a*, *e*, *o*, and *u* with consonant letters in Letter Groups 1–4.
- Mark the vowel in each word with an *x*.
- These are example slides: ta→ vo→ we→ ya→

DECODING

Slides
Mark the slide with an arrow underneath.

tu→   va→

Words
Put an *x* under the vowel in a word.

tub   van
 x   x

A. Mark and say these slides.

te→	va	we	yu	ta	wu
ya	vo	ye	tu	ve	vu

B. Mark the vowels with an *x*.

tax	yam	tan	wax	gum	yes
x					
dug	yum	sun	vet	*fon	*sab

APPLICATION ACTIVITIES

A. Match the uppercase (capital) letter with the lowercase letter.

ReadingHorizons®

Lesson 9 Name Student **Workbook**

Letter Group 4

B. Circle the lowercase letters.

V (x) u Y U w T y W X v t

C. Circle the uppercase (capital) letters.

t (U) W v w T X y V Y u x

D. Match the correct letter with the picture that begins with that letter. The *x* is at the end of the word.

T/t	V/v	W/w	X/x	Y/y	U/u
(ten)	(van)	(web)	(box)	(yarn)	(umbrella)

E. Circle the letter that could be added to make a real word. Use the picture as a clue. Then write the real word, and mark the vowel with an *x*.

1. te__   10   (n) f g   Word: _ten_ (x under e)

2. gu__      d m b   Word: _____

3. fo__      x t p   Word: _____

4. hu__      p x g   Word: _____

5. ve__      t m n   Word: _____

To practice writing the letters in Letter Group 4, go to page 198.

Student **Workbook**   Name

Lesson 10

Letter Group 5

Skills Review

Consonants Q ⌢, Z ⌢⌢, Vowel I ⌢⌢, Consonants C ⊖, K ⊖
- Consonants Q/q, Z/z, C/c, K/k: sound and letter formation.
- In the English language, q has no sound unless it is followed by u. The sound of qu is /kw/.
- Vowel I/i, as in it: sound and letter formation.
- Make slides and build words using the vowels a, e, o, u, and i with consonant letters in Letter Groups 1–5.
- Mark the vowel in each word with an x.
- These are example slides: ke za co qui

DECODING

Slides
Mark the slide with an arrow underneath. Mark the qu with an arc underneath.

ca→   qui→

Words
Put an x under the vowel in a word.

cap   quit
 x   x

A. Mark and say these slides.

| co→ | za | ki | qui | bi | ke |
| ca | que | zi | mi | zo | pi |

B. Mark the vowels with an x.

quip	tax	cut	keg	jig	*kep
x					
dim	cub	fix	kid	zap	*gif

APPLICATION ACTIVITIES

A. Match the uppercase (capital) letter with the lowercase letter.

C   K   Q   Z   I

q   k   i   c   z

(C is connected to c)

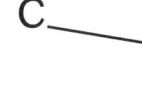

Lesson 10 — Letter Group 5

B. Circle the lowercase letters.

(z) K Q i c Z C k q I

C. Circle the uppercase (capital) letters.

(I) Q k i z K C q Z c

D. Match the correct letter with the picture that begins with that letter.

C/c	K/k	Q/q	Z/z	I/i
(cat)	(kite)	(queen)	(zebra)	(igloo)

E. Circle the letter that could be added to make a real word. Use the picture as a clue. Then write the real word, and mark the vowel with an *x*.

1. ke__    m   b   (g)   Word: _keg_
                                                      x

2. ca__    n   f   g   Word: _____

3. zi__ 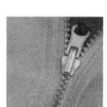   n   p   m   Word: _____

To practice writing the letters in Letter Group 5, go to page 199.

Student **Workbook**   Name

MCW 3

Most Common Words List 3

Skills Review
- Most Common Words are words that are used often when reading and sometimes do not follow phonetic skills.

Most Common Words List 3

one	do	was	were	all	am	from
his	my	there	about	out	me	so

A. Write the missing letters to complete the Most Common Words.

1. h __ s
2. a __ o u __
3. f __ o __
4. w __ __ e
5. o n __
6. a __ l
7. o u __
8. m __
9. t h __ r __
10. s __
11. d __
12. __ y
13. w __ s
14. a __

B. Read the story. Circle the Most Common Words from List 3. Words can be used more than once.

In my class, there are about ten students. We are all from the U.S.

One student is from New York. His name is Dan. He asked me what I do for my job, so I told him I am a cook.

He was a cook in New York before he moved out here. As we talked, we found out that we were cooks at the same restaurant, just in different cities!

Most Common Words List 3

C. Circle the Most Common Word to complete each sentence. Use the sentence as a clue. Then write the word on the line.

1. ep(one)pi (__One__ student is from New York.)

2. bdomkpa (He asked what I _____ for work.)

3. tzwascur (He _____ a cook in New York last year.)

4. leweremip (We _____ cooks at the same restaurant.)

5. hnallfep (We are _____ from the U.S.)

6. ametmil (I _____ a cook.)

7. jempfromt (He is _____ New York.)

8. caebhisp (_____ name is Dan.)

9. nswmybi (He asked what I do for _____ job.)

10. theremrajb (_____ are ten students in my class.)

11. praboutgil (There are _____ ten students in my class.)

12. gakmoutc (He moved _____ here.)

13. vpmebaf (He asked _____ what I do for my job.)

14. wmusorv (He asked me what I do, _____ I told him.)

Student **Workbook**   Name

Lesson 11

Spelling with *C* and *K*

Skills Review
- When the sound /k/ is followed by the vowels *a*, *o*, or *u*, it is spelled with a *c*.
- When the sound /k/ is followed by the vowels *i* or *e*, it is spelled with a *k*.
- Use the rhyme: "*K* takes i *and* e; c *takes the other three*, which are a, o, *and* u."

DECODING

Mark the vowels with an *x* underneath. Notice which vowel follows *c* and which vowel follows *k*.

cup kit
 x   x

A. Mark these *c/k* words.

cop   kid   cat   cog   cup
 x

kin   cut   keg   cab   kit

APPLICATION ACTIVITIES

A. Complete the words with either a *c* or a *k* to make real and nonsense words. Remember that *c* takes *a*, *o*, and *u*, and *k* takes *i* and *e*.
   Example: <u>c</u> **o p.**

1. ___ap   3. ___in   5. *___ep

2. ___it   4. ___ut   6. *___ug

B. Put the *c/k* word in the blank that best completes the sentence. Use the pictures as clues.
   Example: **I like corn on the** <u>cob</u>.
          (cob)   kit   cap

1. Jed will open a _____ of beans.

    can   keg   cad

Lesson 11 — Name — Student **Workbook**

Spelling with *C* and *K*

2. I will use a _____ to drink my milk.

    kin   cup   cog

3. My six year old brother is just a _____.

    Kix   cut   kid

4. A baby bear is a _____.

    cub   kit   cot

Direct and Indirect Quotations

Skills Review
- A direct quotation is when the exact words spoken are written using quotation marks.
- An indirect quotation is when the words spoken have been paraphrased. Quotation marks are not used.

Rules for Using Quotation Marks

Use quotation marks before and after a person's exact words.
  "I have a map," said Mom.

If a person's words are interrupted by other words in a sentence, use quotation marks only around a person's exact words. Use commas to divide the words that are in quotations and the words that are not.
  "In this lab," Dad said, "you will need the mop."
  "This ham is so big," said Tom, "we can all have some."

Capitalize the first word in a quotation, even if it is not the first word in the sentence.
  He said, "The bag will be on the bed."
  Jen asked, "Will you have eggs or ham?"

Use a comma to divide between the spoken words and the person who is saying them. Always put the comma before the quotation marks.
  Bob yelled, "Come here!"
  "This is not for me," Deb said.

Do not capitalize the first word of a quote that has been interrupted, unless the first word begins a new sentence.
  "In this lab," Dad said, "you will need the mop."
  "This ham is so big!" said Tom. "Can we all have some?"

If a quotation ends in a question mark or an exclamation mark, do not use a comma after it to separate the spoken words from the person saying them.
  "Where are you?" Dad asked.
  "I'm in the den!" she called.

Always put a period inside the end quotation mark. Put a question mark or exclamation mark inside the quotation mark if the quotation is a question or exclamation.
  Ben asked, "What should we do?"
  Jen yelled, "I can run!"

Use a new paragraph for every new speaker who is quoted.
  Meg said, "Where is my egg? Oh no! Jed has my egg. Is Jed in the lab? Is Jed in the den? I want my egg!"
  "Oh, no! Meg has my ham!" said Jed. "Do I have her egg? Where is Meg? Is she in the den? I want my ham."

Lesson 12 — Name — Student **Workbook**

 **Direct and Indirect Quotations**

APPLICATION ACTIVITIES

A. Read the sentences. If it is a direct quotation, write *D* for "direct quotation." If it is an indirect quotation, write *I* for "indirect quotation."

Example: **Dad said to go get the map.** _I_

1. Dad said to come to the den. ____

2. "What is in the den?" asked Sam. ____

3. "Your mom wants a map," said Dad. ____

4. Dad said Mom wants to go on a trip. ____

5. "I put the map in the den," said Dad. ____

B. Read the sentences. Add quotation marks to each sentence. Remember to add commas, periods, and question marks.

Example: Dad said come to the den.
                Dad said, "Come to the den."

1. Jan said   Dad and Sam went to get the map

2. Your job   said Dad   is to get this map to mom   Is that OK

3. Can I have Jan help me   asked Sam

4. Dad said   It is OK for Jan and Sam to get the map for Mom

5. Your mom will be so glad   said Dad

Most Common Words List 4

Skills Review
- Most Common Words are words that are used often when reading and sometimes do not follow phonetic skills.

Most Common Words List 4

would	she	very	your	some	go	when
don't	said	good	by	look	too	little

A. Unscramble the letters to form a Most Common Word.

Example: esh __she__

1. doulw _____
2. meso _____
3. ehs _____
4. dasi _____
5. ervy _____
6. kloo _____
7. lettil _____
8. newh _____
9. rouy _____
10. oto _____
11. og _____
12. dogo _____
13. yb _____
14. n'tod _____

B. Read the story. Circle the Most Common Words from List 4. Some words are used more than once.

My sister said she needs to go to the store to get some new pants. I said I would go with her to look but not to buy. I don't have very much money.

When we got to the store, I saw some pants I thought would look good, so I tried them on. They were too little. Then I saw a skirt by the pants that I liked, but my sister said, "Remember, you weren't going to buy anything? You should keep your word." So, I didn't try it on.

Most Common Words List 4

C. Find the Most Common Words from List 4 in the word search. Words can go down ↓, across →, or diagonal ↘ ↗.

```
t  k  b  d  l  d  s  s  h  e  b
o  s  o  t  l  i  m  a  t  f  y
o  o  n  u  b  i  t  u  i  r  l
g  o  o  s  o  m  e  t  u  d  o
d  w  v  e  r  y  k  o  l  x  o
w  h  e  n  u  o  y  r  d  e  k
```

would   some   said   too   she   go   good
little   very   when   by   your   don't look

D. Circle the Most Common Word to correctly complete each sentence. Then write the word on the line.

1. I said I _____ go. (would/when)

2. _____ needs some pants. (She/Look)

3. The pants look _____ good. (don't/very)

4. You should keep _____ word. (your/by)

5. She needs _____ pants. (go/some)

6. She needs to _____ to the store. (go/your)

7. I saw some pants _____ we got to the store. (when/don't)

8. I _____ have very much money. (don't/look)

9. I _____ I didn't have money. (very/said)

10. I think the pants look _____. (good/too)

11. It is _____ the pants. (some/by)

12. Those pants _____ good. (would/look)

13. The pants are _____ little. (said/too)

14. The skirt was not too _____. (little/when)

Student **Workbook**   Name

Lesson 13

Alphabetical Order

Skills Review
- This is the alphabet in alphabetical order: a b c d e f g h i j k l m n o p q r s t u v w x y z
- Alphabetical order is a necessary skill in order to use a dictionary, phone book, etc.

APPLICATION ACTIVITIES

A. Write the matching lowercase or uppercase (capital) letter next to each letter.

A _a_   _B_ b   C ___   D ___

___ e   F ___   ___ g   H ___

___ i   J ___   ___ k   L ___

M ___   ___ n   O ___   ___ p

Q ___   ___ r   ___ s   T ___

___ u   V ___   W ___   ___ x

Y ___   ___ z

B. Write the correct lowercase or uppercase (capital) letter in alphabetical order.

1.   _a_ , b, c, ___

2.   ___ , t, ___ , v

3.   W, ___ , Y, ___

4.   n, ___ , p, ___ , r

5.   E, ___ , G, ___ , I

6.   ___ , K, ___ M

ReadingHorizons®

Lesson 13 — Name — Student **Workbook**

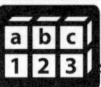
Alphabetical Order

C. Rewrite the words in alphabetical order.

1. fan   big   hat

     a) _____big_____
     b) _____fan_____
     c) _____hat_____

2. wax   tan   fog

     a) _____
     b) _____
     c) _____

3. sad   not   mad

     a) _____
     b) _____
     c) _____

4. box   tag   pit

     a) _____
     b) _____
     c) _____

5. can   sit   fox

     a) _____
     b) _____
     c) _____

Articles

Skills Review

- Articles are used before nouns. These are articles: *a, an, the*.
- *A* and *an* are used to refer to something that is not specific (*This is a hat.; It is an old hat.*).
- *The* is used to refer to a specific thing or person (*The hat is red.*).
- Use *a* if the word following the article begins with a consonant or has a consonant sound (*a hat*).
- Use *an* if the word following the article begins with a vowel or a vowel sound (*an ant*).
- Exceptions: If the first consonant of the word is silent and the vowel is heard, use the article *an* (*an hour*). If the word begins with a long *u* vowel sound, use the article *a* (*a unit*).

APPLICATION ACTIVITIES

A. Read these words. Do the words begin with a consonant sound or a vowel sound? Write *a* or *an* before each word.

1. _a_ box
2. _____ cat
3. _____ pet
4. _____ elf
5. _____ rat
6. _____ ox
7. _____ pan
7. _____ fox
9. _____ mop
10. _____ ax
11. _____ dog
12. _____ ant
13. _____ fan
14. _____ egg
15. _____ van
16. _____ bed

B. Complete the sentences. Write *a* or *an*.

1. _A_ cat is _an_ animal.
   a.   b.

2. _____ apple is _____ fruit.
   a.   b.

3. _____ dog is _____ pet.
   a.   b.

4. _____ van is _____ car.
   a.   b.

5. Soccer is _____ sport.

6. She is _____ student.

7. Africa is _____ country.

8. _____ ant is _____ insect.
   a.   b.

 **Articles**

C. Look at the pictures. Complete the sentences with *the*, *a*, or *an*. Fill in the first blank with *the*. Fill in the second blank with *a* or *an*.

1. Who are they?
   girl   man

   a. _The_ girl is _a_ student.   b. _The_ man is _a_ teacher.

2. What are they?
   dog   cat

   a. _____ dog is _____ puppy.   b. _____ cat is _____ kitten.

3. What are they?
   fly   elephant

   a. _____ fly is _____ insect.   b. _____ elephant is _____ animal.

4. What are they?
   apple   carrot

   a. _____ apple is _____ fruit.   b. _____ carrot is _____ vegetable.

5. Which one is a planet?
   Earth   Sun

   a. _____ Earth is _____ planet.   b. _____ Sun is not _____ planet.

Student **Workbook** Name

Reading in Context

Chapter 1

Practice reading this tag using all the skills you've learned in Chapter 1. Review the words that are difficult for you. Then read the tag to a teacher or friend.

Your Little Red Pot

In this Kit:
- one little red pot
- one box of mud
- one mat

About this pot:
- It can fit one cup of mud.
- If it is too hot, get it out of the sun.
- If it is wet, set it on a mat.

Reading in Context

Practice reading this blog using all the skills you've learned in Chapter 1. Review the words that are difficult for you. Then read the blog to a teacher or friend.

My Blog

My cat Tom got hit by a van. His hip and leg are bad, so we will go to the vet. She will look at his hip and leg. She will get out her kit and say, "I can fix that." We will be in and out. She is a good vet, and Tom is a good pet.

Student **Workbook**   Name

Lesson 15

L-Blends

Skills Review
Blends
- A Blend is two or three consonants that stand together.
- Each letter keeps its own sound.
- A Blend must be able to begin a word.
- A Blend contains *l*, *r*, or *s*. Exceptions are *dw* and *tw*.

Skills Review
L-Blends
- *L*-Blends have an *l* in it.
- The *l* stands with another consonant.
- The *l* is the second letter in the Blend.
- These are the *l*-Blends: bl cl fl gl pl sl

DECODING

Mark Blends with an arc underneath, like this:

bl   blog

A. Mark the Blends.

bl   cl   fl   gl   pl   sl

B. Mark the words.

blog   club   flat   glad   plan   slip

READING

Read these sentences. Notice the words that have *l*-Blends.

This is Cliff. He has a sled. He is glad the land is not flat. He plans to have a blast.

L-Blends

APPLICATION ACTIVITIES

A. Write the *l*-Blends.

This is C l iff. He has a __ __ed. He is __ __ad the land is not __ __at. He __ __ans to have a __ __ast.

B. Circle the *l*-Blends.

(bl)   cl   dl   fl   gl   hl   kl   nl   pl   rl   sl   tl   wl

C. Change the letter to make a new word that rhymes.
   Example: plan: p → c = _clan_

1. **flip:** f → c = _____
2. **clap:** c → s = _____
3. **plot:** p → b = _____
4. **bled:** b → f = _____
5. **slam:** s → c = _____
6. **glob:** g → s = _____

D. Write the *l*-Blend word under the picture. Use the words in the box.

| plug | glad | flag |
| sled | clap | black |

  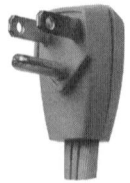 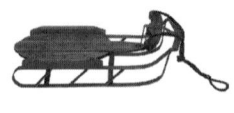  

Student **Workbook** Name

Lesson 16

Double S, F, and Z

Skills Review
- In single-syllable words that end in the sound of *s*, *f*, or *z*, the ending consonant is usually doubled.
- There are 21 exceptions: *is*, *as*, *his*, *has*, *was*, *gas*, *bus*, *yes*, *us*, *plus*, *pus*, *this*, *goes*, *does*, *says*, *if*, *of*, *clef*, *chef*, *whiz*, and *quiz*.
- An easy way to remember the skill is to make up an acronym (**S**an **F**rancisco **Z**oo).

A. Add another consonant to complete these words.

1. kis_s_
2. clas__
3. fluf__
4. fiz__
5. buz__
6. clif__
7. jaz__
8. bles__
9. puf__
10. fus__
11. cuf__
12. raz__

B. Now rewrite the words in Activity A.

1. _kiss_
2. _____
3. _____
4. _____
5. _____
6. _____
7. _____
8. _____
9. _____
10. _____
11. _____
12. _____

READING

Read these sentences. Notice the words that have double *s*, *f*, and *z*.

Cliff sits in the grass. The bugs buzz. He has a can of pop. He takes off the top, and it goes, "Fizz!"

Lesson 16   Name   Student **Workbook**

 **Double S, F, and Z**

APPLICATION ACTIVITIES

A. Write the missing letters.

Cli _f_ _f_ sits in the gra__ __. The bugs bu__ __. He has a can of pop. He takes o__ __ the top, and it goes, "Fi__ __!"

B. Choose the correct ending in the box to make words. Write the ending to form the words.

| ss | ff | zz |

1. The bugs bu _z_ _z_.

2. His name is Cli__ __.

3. The pop goes fi__ __.

4. He takes o__ __ the top.

5. He sits in the gra__ __.

C. Circle the word that rhymes with the first word.

1. **puff:** (cuff)   pass   fizz   cliff

2. **bliss:** class   miss   fizz   bluff

3. **glass:** puff   jazz   bliss   class

4. **mass:** pass   mess   buzz   fluff

5. **buff:** bass   bluff   cliff   fizz

6. **jazz:** fuzz   bass   razz   cuff

Student Workbook Name _____ Lesson 17

Special Vowel Combinations: -LL, -NG, -NK

Skills Review

-LL:
- When vowels are followed by a double *l* in single-syllable words, some of the vowel sounds change.
- The *-ll* Special Vowel Combinations are: *-all, -ell, -oll, -ull, -ill*.
- The *-all* vowel sound changes. Examples: *call, fall, mall*.
- The *-oll* vowel sound changes. Examples: *roll, toll, troll* (exceptions are *doll* and *loll*).
- The *-ull* has two slightly different sounds. Examples: *gull* vs. *pull*; *dull* vs. *bull*.

-NG, -NK:
- When vowels are followed by the consonants *-ng* or *-nk* in single-syllable words, some of the vowel sounds change.
- The *-ng* Special Vowel Combinations are: *-ang, -ing, -ong, -ung*.
- The *-nk* Special Vowel Combinations are: *-ank, -ink, -onk, -unk*.
- The new sound for *-ang* and *-ank*: the *a* sound is long. Examples: *bang; rang; sank; tank*.
- The new sound for *-ing* and *-ink*: the *i* has the sound of long *e*. Examples: *ring; cling; pink; sink*.
- There are only two single-syllable words with *-eng* (*length, strength*).
- There are no words spelled with *-enk*.

DECODING

-LL:
- Mark the vowel with an *x*, and arc the vowel and *ll* together to make the sound.

-NG, -NK:
- Mark the vowel with an *x*, and arc the vowel and *ng/nk* together to make the sound.

A. Mark these words.

tall   wink   sing   fill   honk

sang   well   blink   full   song

READING

Read these sentences. Notice the words that have Special Vowel Combinations.

| Bill, call all the men who still want to buy my big bull. If all goes well, we may sell it! | Jill was asked to sing for the king! She filled her lungs. As she sang, the notes rang out long and strong and hung in the air. |

Lesson 17   Name   Student **Workbook**

Special Vowel Combinations: -LL, -NG, -NK

> Honk! Honk!
> Jill came out in her pink tank top and sank into her seat.
> Hank put her case in the trunk.
> "Let's stop at the bank!" she said with a wink.

APPLICATION ACTIVITIES

A. Answer the questions about the reading passages above using words from the sentences.

1. What was Bill selling? _____

2. What was Jill asked to do? _____

3. Where did Jill want to go? _____

B. (Circle) all of the words that rhyme with the first word listed.
Example: bill: (gill) (dill) ball (hill)

1. **sink:**	link	hang	wink	blink
2. **well:**	sell	tell	swell	full
3. **tall:**	call	fall	poll	ball
4. **junk:**	tank	bunk	dunk	sunk
5. **sang:**	rang	fang	bang	sung
6. **ring:**	sing	wing	rang	fling

C. Find and circle these words that contain Special Vowel Combinations in the word search. Words can go down ↓, across →, or diagonal ↘ ↗.

bank	long	sing
fall	lung	sink
full	rang	tell
honk	rink	will
junk	roll	toll

```
l z m r b a n k l
w a g o f u l l m
h i i l k z e u j
t o l l j t n f u
r i n l n l u h n
y n o k l f o v k
s i n k u a w n k
s i n g n l j n g
r r a n g l l s e
```

44   **Reading**Horizons®

Student *Workbook*   Name

Most Common Words List 5

Skills Review
- Most Common Words are words that are used often when reading and sometimes do not follow phonetic skills.

Most Common Words List 5

where	then	every	what	no	or	know
their	see	which	any	like	people	into

A. Read the story. Circle the Most Common Words from List 5.

I know a lot of people, but I also like to meet new people every day on the bus.

I ask people questions such as, "Where are you from?" and "What do you do?" I also ask which kinds of movies they like to go see. Then I ask how many people are in their family or if they have any kids.

I have no problem getting into a conversation with people when I ask them things about themselves.

B. Write the missing letters to complete the Most Common Words.

1. k __ o __
2. t h __ __ r
3. __ n t __
4. e v __ r __
5. w h __ __
6. a __ y
7. __ h __ c __
8. w __ __ r e
9. p __ o p __ e
10. __ o
11. t __ __ n
12. s __ __
13. __ r
14. l i __ __

Most Common Words List 5

C. One of the words in each set is a Most Common Word, and the other is a nonsense word. Circle the Most Common Word.

Example: (into) toin

1. know   wokn
2. ees   see
3. people   opelpe
4. any   yna
5. chiwh   which
6. neth   then
7. what   tawh
8. every   yrvee
9. erehw   where
10. or   oir
11. otni   into
12. leik   like
13. threi   their
14. ni   no

Student Workbook Name

Lesson 18

R-Blends

Skills Review
- *R*-Blends have an *r* in them.
- The *r* stands with another consonant.
- The *r* is the second letter in the Blend.
- These are the *r*-Blends: br cr dr fr gr pr tr

DECODING

Mark Blends with an arc underneath.

br   brag

A. Mark the *r*-Blends.

br   cr   dr   fr   gr   pr   tr

B. Read these *r*-Blend slides.

bra   cre   dri   fro   gra   pre   tri

C. Mark these words that have *r*-Blends.

bran   crop   drip   from   grab   *briff

grip   prom   trip   drum   frog   *tran

READING

Read these sentences. Notice the words that have *r*-Blends.

This is Brad. He has a pet frog and crab. He drops them in the grass and prods them to trot.

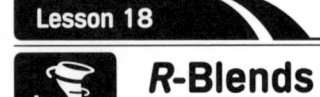

R-Blends

APPLICATION ACTIVITIES

A. Write the *r*-Blends.

This is _B_ _r_ ad. He has a pet __ __og and __ __ab. He __ __ops them in the grass and __ __ods them to __ __ot.

B. Circle the *r*-Blends.

br   cr   dr   fr   gr   hr   kr   lr   nr   pr   sr   tr   vr

C. Change the *l*-Blends to *r*-Blends to make a new word that rhymes.
Example: slap: sl → tr = _trap_

1. clip: cl → gr = _____

2. plum: pl → dr = _____

3. plan: pl → br = _____

4. clap: cl → tr = _____

5. slab: sl → cr = _____

6. plop: pl → pr = _____

Student Workbook Name _____

Lesson 19

Plurals

Skills Review
- When there are two or more of an item or thing, it is called a *plural*.
- An *s* is added to words ending in a consonant (two *hats*, three *pigs*, five *pens*).
- The sound of the plural *s* changes from /s/ if the ending consonant is *voiceless* (ha*t*s) to /z/ if it is *voiced* (pe*n*s). (The letters between slash marks "/ /" represent sounds.)
- If a word ends in *ss*, *zz*, or *x*, the *es* plural must be added. The sound for *es* is /iz/ (dress*es*, buzz*es*, box*es*). Plural forms of nouns that end in *y* will be addressed later.

DECODING

Underline the plural ending.

hat<u>s</u>   box<u>es</u>

A. Underline the plural ending in these words.

trap<u>s</u>   classes   lids   legs

dresses   frogs   boxes   cats

B. Rewrite the word with the plural ending.

1. clap ___claps___   5. mat _____

2. clam _____   6. glass _____

3. dog _____   7. pad _____

4. kiss _____   8. fox _____

READING

Read this sentence. Notice the plural words.

Jen put her hat, cups, mats, rug, pans, and dresses in a big box.

Lesson 19 — Plurals

Student Workbook

APPLICATION ACTIVITIES

A. Answer the question about the reading on the previous page.

1. What did Jen put in a big box? _____

_____

B. Match the words with the correct picture. The first one is done for you.

1. mat
2. cups
3. hats
4. rug
5. pans
6. dress
7. boxes

C. What is the correct ending sound of the plural endings? Write each word in the correct column.

<s>boxes</s>   classes   hat<u>s</u>   cap<u>s</u>   pen<u>s</u>   frog<u>s</u>
buzz<u>es</u>   cuff<u>s</u>   leg<u>s</u>   dress<u>es</u>   cat<u>s</u>   pig<u>s</u>

/s/	/z/	/iz/
		box<u>es</u>

Student **Workbook**   Name

Lesson 20
Possessives

Skills Review
- A possessive identifies who or what *has* something or to whom something belongs.
- To make a *singular noun* possessive, add an apostrophe and *s* (*'s*).
- A *plural noun* that does not end with an *s* is made possessive by adding the apostrophe *s* (*'s*).
- Add just the apostrophe to *plural nouns* ending with *s* (*s'*).
- Like plurals, the sound of the possessive is /s/, /z/, or /iz/, depending on the ending consonant. Examples: Pa*t's* = /s/; Je*n's* = /z/; Je*ss's* = /ez/. (The letters between slash marks "/ /" represent sounds.)

DECODING

There are no decoding rules for possessives. Use the following rules for adding apostrophes.

To make a *singular noun* possessive, add an apostrophe and an *s* (*'s*). (Example: <u>Jen's</u> hat is in the box.)

> Jen's

A *plural noun* that does not end with an *s* is made possessive by adding the apostrophe *s* (*'s*). (Example: Did you shine the <u>men's</u> shoes?)

> men's

Add just the apostrophe to *plural nouns* ending with *s* (*s'*). (Example: Those are the <u>kids'</u> hats.)

> kids'

A. Make these words possessive by adding an apostrophe *s* (*'s*).

dog's   Jeff   men   class

fox   cop   cub   jet

B. Make these plural words possessive by adding just an apostrophe (').

cats'   frogs   pigs   foxes

classes   jets   cubs   cops

Lesson 20 — Name — Student **Workbook**

Possessives

C. What is the sound of the possessive ending in the words from Activities A and B? Write the words you formed in Activities A and B in the correct columns.

/s/	/z/	/iz/

READING

Read these sentences. Notice the possessive nouns.

What is Tim's plan? What is Fred's plan? What is the students' plan? Will it be the men's plan?

APPLICATION ACTIVITIES

A. Write 's or s' for the possessive nouns from the reading above.

What is Tim____ plan? What is Fred____ plan? What is the student____ plan? Will it be the men____ plan?
         1.   2.
                  3.   4.

B. Match the words with the correct picture. The first one is done for you.

1. man's job
2. men's jobs
3. kid's dog
4. kids' dog
5. class's bus
6. classes' buses

Student Workbook Name _____

Lesson 21

S-Blends

Skills Review
- S-Blends have an *s* in them.
- The *s* stands with another consonant.
- The *s* is the *first* letter in the Blend.
- Some *s*-Blends can begin <u>and</u> end words.
- These are the two-letter *s*-Blends: <u>sc</u> <u>sk</u> <u>sl</u> <u>sm</u> <u>sn</u> <u>sp</u> <u>st</u> <u>sw</u>
- These are the three-letter *s*-Blends: <u>scr</u> <u>spr</u> <u>str</u> <u>spl</u> <u>squ</u>

DECODING

Mark Blends with an arc underneath.

sc   scan_x   st   best_x

A. Mark the *s*-Blends.

sc   sk   sl   sm   sn   sp   st

sw   scr   spr   str   spl   squ

B. Read these *s*-Blend slides.

sca   ske   slo   sme   snu   stre   squi

spo   sti   swa   scru   spri   spla

C. Mark these words that have *s*-Blends. Remember to mark the Special Vowel Combinations.

scan   skin   slip   smell   squid

snob   spill   stop   swim   task

scrap   spring   strong   split   clasp

Lesson 21 — Name — Student **Workbook**

 **S-Blends**

READING

Read these sentences. Notice the words that have s-Blends.

Every year, Scott likes to stop at a small spot in a spring. He has good swim skills that keep him strong and slim.

APPLICATION ACTIVITIES

A. Write the s-Blends from the sentences above.

Every year, __ __ott likes to __ __op at a __ __all __ __ott in a __ __ __ing. He has good __ __im __ __ills that keep him __ __ __ong and __ __im.

B. Circle the s-Blends.

(sc) sd sk sl sm sn sp sr st sv sw

scr sdr sfr spr str spl svl squ

C. Change the l- and r-Blends to s-Blends to make a new word that rhymes.
   Example: trap: tr → str = _strap_

1. slap: sl → scr = _____
2. bring: br → spr = _____
3. dress: dr → str = _____
4. slit: sl → spl = _____
5. grid: gr → squ = _____
6. prop: pr → st = _____

D. Is the spelling sc- or sk-? Write sc- or sk- to correctly complete the word. Remember the c/k rule.

1. __ __in
2. __ __an
3. __ __im
4. __ __ab
5. __ __id
6. __ __am
7. __ __ip
8. __ __uff
9. __ __at
10. *__ __eb
11. *__ __ob
12. *__ __izz

Student Workbook Name

Lesson 22

Two Extra Blends

Skills Review
- A Blend has to be able to *begin* a word.
- There are not many words that use the extra Blends.
- *Qu* is not a Blend but is marked like a Blend.
- These are the two extra Blends: dw tw

DECODING

Mark Blends with an arc underneath. Mark *qu* like a Blend.

dw   dwell   qu   quit

tw   twig

A. Mark these Blends.

dw   tw

B. Read these slides.

twi   dwe   twe   dwi

C. Mark these words.

twin   twill   dwell   quit

*quep   *dwip   *twed   *queb

*dwut   twist   quill   *dwed

READING

Read these sentences. Notice the words that have Blends.

Dan yanks and twists the twig. He and his twin, Jan, had to trim all of the plants.

Lesson 22 Name   Student **Workbook**

 **Two Extra Blends**

APPLICATION ACTIVITIES

A. Write the extra Blends.

Dan yanks and __ __ists the __ __ig. He and his __ __in, Jan, had to trim all of the plants.

B. Circle the Blends. There are 11.

br   bs   cl   dr   dw   fr   sc   sd   sn

sv   sw   sdr   sfr   str   svl   squ   stw   tw

C. Change the Blends to make a new word that rhymes.
Example: trap: tr → str = _strap_

1. grin: gr → tw = _____
2. spell: sp → dw = _____
3. trig: tr → tw = _____
4. drill: dr → qu = _____
5. grill: gr → tw = _____
6. spit: sp → qu = _____

D. Unscramble the words with extra Blends to make real words. Use the definitions as clues.

1. wgti   __ __ O __
Hint: a small branch from a tree (rhymes with *big*)

2. wldel   __ O __ __ __
Hint: to live (rhymes with *bell*)

3. tiwn   O __ __ __
Hint: two brothers or sisters (or a brother and a sister) that were born at the same time (rhymes with *grin*)

4. tillw   O __ __ __ __
Hint: a kind of cloth (rhymes with *bill*)

E. Take the letters that appear in the circles (O), and unscramble them for the final word.

____ ____ ____ _s_ ____
Hint: to turn or bend (rhymes with *list*)

Student Workbook Name

MCW 6

Most Common Words List 6

Skills Review
- Most Common Words are words that are used often when reading and sometimes do not follow phonetic skills.

Most Common Words List 6

| down | many | year | has | around | saw | how |
| been | could | them | come | put | than | now |

A. Read the story. Circle the Most Common Words from List 6.

Every year, I like to do something fun for my birthday. (It helps me to forget how old I am!)

I have done many fun things in the past. Last year, I put on my nice dress and saw a play down on the town.

This year my family will come visit me. Now that I live in California, I could take them around to my favorite beaches. My mom has never been to a beach! My birthday will be even better than last year!

B. Unscramble the letters to form a Most Common Word.
Example: wno __now__

1. tup _____
2. mthe _____
3. dounra _____
4. reay _____
5. yanm _____
6. bnee _____
7. hwo _____
8. nath _____
9. sha _____
10. nwo _____
11. cemo _____
12. cuodl _____
13. swa _____
14. wodn _____

Most Common Words List 6

C. Circle the correct Most Common Word to complete each sentence. Then write the word on the line.
Example: I _have_ a hat. (**have**/be)

1. Put it _____ on the table. (down/many)

2. I have _____ friends. (now/many)

3. Last _____ I went to a play. (year/come)

4. My mom _____ never been to the beach. (has/around)

5. I will take them _____ the town. (put/around)

6. I _____ a play last year. (saw/how)

7. _____ old are you? (Them/How)

8. My mom has never _____ to a beach. (down/been)

9. I _____ take them to the beach. (been/could)

10. Can you _____? (come/could)

11. I _____ on my dress. (saw/put)

12. This year will be better _____ last year. (than/down)

13. I live in California _____. (now/year)

14. I could take _____ to the beach. (them/than)

Reading in Context

Practice reading this advertisement using all the skills you've learned in Chapter 2. Review the words that are difficult for you. Then read the advertisement to a teacher or friend.

Red Prom Dress Must Sell!

$75 or less

Like to twist and swing? Then this is the dress for you!

10 tall · got it this year · has a slim look · pink trim on top · brass clasps · small rips on strap · very glam

Call Fran King, 412-555-9041

Reading in Context

Practice reading this restaurant review using all the skills you've learned in Chapter 2. Review the words that are difficult for you. Then read the review to a teacher or friend.

Review

At Greg's Grill Pit, the grub is hot, but the jazz is not.

Greg's Grill Pit is a small club by the bank. When you go in, you will see a big tank of crabs and squid. When you sit down, they will bring you a tall drink and the best crab dip around. If you are not full yet, you can get king crab legs or squid, crisp and hot off the grill. As for the jazz, the club is too small for drums and brass. But the grub is good. What to do? Get it to go!

Student **Workbook** Name

Short and Long Vowels

Lesson 23

Skills Review
- All vowels have more than one sound.
- Vowels are marked with markings to show the vowel sound in a word.
- Vowel markings tell whether the vowel is short (the sound of the vowel) or long (the name of the vowel).
- These are the markings: short vowel = ˘, long vowel = ¯.

DECODING

To show that a vowel sound is short, put a "˘" above the vowel.

ă ĕ ŏ ŭ ĭ

To show that a vowel sound is long, put a "¯" above the vowel.

ā ē ō ū ī

A. Mark these vowels short by putting a "˘" above the vowel.

a   e   o   u   i

B. Mark these vowels long by putting a "¯" above the vowel.

a   e   o   u   i

APPLICATION ACTIVITIES

A. Write these short vowel words and long vowel words under the correct vowel sound. Have someone read the words to you if needed. Pay attention to the sounds of the vowels.

| cute | ten | pay | up | kid |
| can | be | off | go | hi |

Short Vowels

ă	ĕ	ŏ	ŭ	ĭ

Long Vowels

ā	ē	ō	ū	ī

ReadingHorizons®

Short and Long Vowels

B. (Circle) the short vowel slides. <u>Underline</u> the long vowel slides. Read the slides.

(tă)   nē   kĕ   rō   bŭ

cā   pŏ   mĭ   dū   fī

C. Find and circle these short vowel words in the word search. Words can go down ↓, across →, or diagonal ↘ ↗.

```
m  s  l  b  k  g
j  s  g  e  d  s
o  i  c  d  q  r
b  t  p  u  s  p
c  a  t  e  u  f
d  o  g  c  n  i
```

bag   big   cup   job   sit
bed   cat   dog   pen   sun

Student **Workbook**   Name

Lesson 24

Phonetic Skill 1

Skills Review
- When a vowel is followed by one guardian consonant, the vowel sound is *short*.
- The term *guardian consonant* is used to identify the consonant following the vowel and to distinguish it from other consonants in a word.
- A guardian consonant is marked with a *guardian star* (*).

DECODING

To prove the word:
1. Move *under* the word left to right. Place an *x* under the vowel. If there is a blend in the word, mark it with an arc. (If a blend begins the word, arc it before marking the vowel.)
2. Continue moving to the right and see if there is a guardian consonant (and nothing else) following the vowel. Move up and mark the guardian consonant with a guardian star (*).
3. Move left to the vowel. Mark the vowel short with the short vowel mark (⌣). The guardian consonant makes the vowel short.

stŏp*   măn*

A. Mark the guardian consonant with a guardian star (*).

hat   bed   rug   kid

B. Prove these words.

mom   box   big   step

run   quit   plan   nut

READING

Read these signs. Notice the Phonetic Skill 1 words.

Lesson 24 — Phonetic Skill 1

APPLICATION ACTIVITIES

A. Write the word from the box next to the word it rhymes with.

| cup | trip | plus | pen | drop | *kep |

1. men _____   4. step _____

2. stop _____   5. bus _____

3. up _____   6. dip _____

B. Change the vowel to make a new word.
Example: cat: a → u = __cut__

1. hug: u → o = _____   4. tip: i → a = _____

2. man: a → e = _____   5. hat: a → i = _____

3. cop: o → u = _____   6. bed: e → a = _____

C. Circle the three words that rhyme.

1. **bad:** mad   big   glad   get   sad   lid

2. **fit:** fun   it   split   lip   mat   hit

Student Workbook

Phonetic Skill 2

Skills Review
- When a vowel is followed by two guardian consonants, the vowel sound is *short*.
- Blends can come at the end of the word. Mark them with two guardian stars because you hear two sounds.

DECODING

To mark and prove the word:
1. Move *under* the word left to right. Place an *x* under the vowel. If a Blend begins the word, arc it before marking the vowel.
2. Continue moving to the right. Note that there are *two* guardian consonants. Move up and around, and mark each consonant with a guardian star.
3. Move left to the vowel. Mark the vowel short with the short vowel mark (˘). The *two* guardian consonants make the vowel sound short.

    hint   blend

A. Mark each guardian consonant with a guardian star (*). Remember that when Blends are guardians, they each get a guardian star.

last   help   soft   must   milk

B. Prove these words. Be sure to mark Blends.

list   send   next   stand

ask   cost   dust   lift

READING

Read this ad. Notice the Phonetic Skill 2 words.

WANT TO SPEND LESS ON RENT? Let us help you! Well-kept condo for rent in west end of town. Cost: $800 per month. This is the best deal in town. Act fast! This won't last long! You must see it to believe it!

Lesson 25 — Name — Student **Workbook**

Phonetic Skill 2

APPLICATION ACTIVITIES

A. List four words that follow Phonetic Skill 2 from the ad on the previous page.

1. _____   3. _____

2. _____   4. _____

B. Write the Phonetic Skill 2 words that rhyme.

| land | twist | fast | send | best | dust |
| past | rest | spend | just | mist | band |

1. last   _____   _____

2. trust _____   _____

3. end   _____   _____

4. test   _____   _____

5. sand   _____   _____

6. list   _____   _____

C. Add the two final consonants to form the word in the picture.

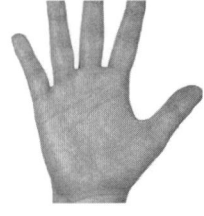  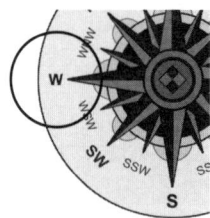 

h a __ __   l a __ __   w e __ __   p l a __ __

D. Write a sentence using one of the words from Activity C.

_____

_____

Student Workbook

Lesson 26

Vowel Families *O* and *I*
-old -ind

Skills Review
- When two consonants follow the vowels *o* or *i*, sometimes the vowel sound will be long. We call these *vowel families*. These are the vowel families: *-old*, *-olt*, *-ost*, *-ind*, *-ild*.

DECODING

Mark the vowel with an *x*. Underline the vowel family. Then mark the vowel long.

ōlt   īnd

bōlt   fīnd

A. Mark the vowel families.

ōld   olt   ost   ind   ild

B. Prove the words.

hōld   jolt   most   grind   mild

scold   volt   host   mind   wild

READING

Read the Web site article. Notice the words that contain Vowel Families *O* and *I*.

The Perfect Home

Old homes were hard to find, but Mike knew just what he had in mind. He checked the list of ads in the paper every day. At last, he found one that had been well cared for. Time had not taken its toll on this home. He couldn't even find any mold! Mike knew it was the kind of home he wanted, so he told the realtor to hold it for him.

ReadingHorizons®

Lesson 26 Name

Vowel Families O and I

APPLICATION ACTIVITIES

A. Write three words from the article on the previous page that rhyme with *old*. Write two words from the article that rhyme with *find*.

1. old: _____   2. find: _____

   _____   _____

   _____

B. Write the word from the box that correctly completes the sentence. Use the rhyming word at the end of the sentence as a clue. Then read the sentence.

| host | bolt | wild | gold | kind |

1. Did he find the _____? (told)

2. The horse is _____. (mild)

3. She was _____ to me. (mind)

4. The _____ of lightning hit the box. (colt)

5. I will thank the _____ before I go. (most)

C. Unscramble the letters to make words with vowel families *o* and *i*.

1. tolv _____   3. ldim _____   5. lsod _____

2. dnim _____   4. tpos _____

Student **Workbook**   Name   Lesson 27

Parts of Speech

Skills Review
- A *noun* names a person, place, thing, or idea. (Example: The <u>bus</u> is big.)
- An *adjective* describes a noun. (Example: It is a <u>big</u> bus.)
- A *verb* names an action or state. (Example: I <u>sit</u> on the bus.)
- An *adverb* describes a verb, an adjective, or another adverb. Frequently, adverbs end in the suffix *-ly*. (Example: I <u>quickly</u> get on the bus.)

A. Circle the nouns. <u>Underline</u> the adjectives. Use the sentences as clues.

(hat)   <u>red</u>   rug   kid   cat

big   bed   old   dog   small

1. He has a big dog.
2. She has a small cat.
3. She has a red hat.
4. That rug is old.
5. The kid is in bed.

B. Read the sentences. Circle the verbs.

1. (Ask) your mom.
2. Help me!
3. Don't spend more than $5.
4. Mix the egg and milk.
5. I swim in the pond.

Parts of Speech

C. Change these adjectives to adverbs by adding the suffix *-ly*.
   Example: **quick (-ly) quickly**

1. slow (-ly) _____

2. soft (-ly) _____

3. loud (-ly) _____

4. bad (-ly) _____

5. sad (-ly) _____

6. glad (-ly) _____

Student **Workbook** Name Lesson 28

Adding Suffixes to Phonetic Skills 1 and 2

Skills Review
- A *suffix* is one or more letters added to the end of a word.
- Sometimes, adding a suffix to a word makes a new word or changes the part of speech.
- To add the suffixes *-ing*, *-ed*, *-er*, and *-est* to Phonetic Skill 1 words, double the consonant before adding the ending.
- To add the suffixes *-ing*, *-ed*, *-er*, and *-est* to Phonetic Skill 2 words, words that end in *x*, and words that end in Special Vowel Combinations, just add the suffix.

DECODING

To prove words with suffixes:
1. Prove the base word.
2. Rewrite the word with the suffix. (Check for two consonants before adding the suffix.)
3. Underline the suffix.

hop   hopp<u>ing</u>   test   test<u>ed</u>

A. Underline the suffix in each word.

clapp<u>ing</u>   bumped   lifting   biggest   smaller

B. Prove the base word. Rewrite the word with the suffix. Then underline the suffix.
   Example: sit (-ing) sitt<u>ing</u>

1. h i t (-ing) _____   4. b u z z (-ing) _____

2. p l a n t (-er) _____ 5. f a t (-est) _____

3. r u s t (-ed) _____   6. f i x (-ing) _____

READING

Read the letter. Notice the Phonetic Skill 1 and Phonetic Skill 2 words with suffixes.

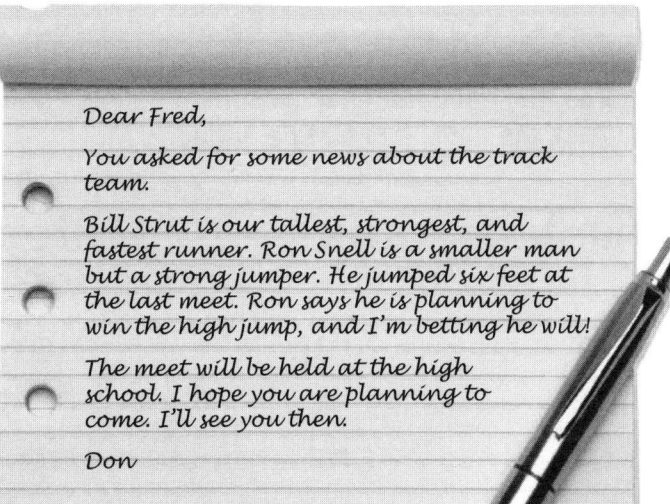

Dear Fred,

You asked for some news about the track team.

Bill Strut is our tallest, strongest, and fastest runner. Ron Snell is a smaller man but a strong jumper. He jumped six feet at the last meet. Ron says he is planning to win the high jump, and I'm betting he will!

The meet will be held at the high school. I hope you are planning to come. I'll see you then.

Don

Lesson 28 — Name _____ — Student **Workbook**

 **Adding Suffixes to Phonetic Skills 1 and 2**

APPLICATION ACTIVITIES

A. Write the base word for each word with a suffix.
   Example: **hopping** _hop_

1. winning _____
2. fastest _____
3. stronger _____
4. smallest _____
5. jumped _____
6. taller _____
7. running _____
8. planned _____

B. Complete the sentences with the correct word.

| clapped | smaller | hottest | dusting | camping |

1. This summer is the _____ one in years.

2. The maid is _____ the lamp with a rag.

3. Jed is _____ in the hills with a tent.

4. Ned _____ at the end of the show.

5. My cat is _____ than your cat.

C. Draw a (circle) around the words that need the final consonant doubled before adding -*ing*, -*ed*, -*er*, or -*est*. Underline the words in which the suffix can just be added.

(flat)   hunt   fix   stop   bend

snag   spit   limp   plot   tend

stuff   plan   sift   trip   set

Student **Workbook** Name   Lesson 29

Three Sounds of -ED

Skills Review
- The suffix *-ed* has three sounds. The sound of the consonant that immediately precedes *-ed* determines the correct pronunciation of the suffix *-ed*.
- Following voiceless letters (⊖) (such as *f, k, p, s, x*), the sound is /t/ (*kicked*).
- Following voiced letters (ⓌⓌ) (such as *n, m, b, g, v, l, z,* and vowels), the sound is /d/ (*sobbed*).
- When words end in *t* or *d*, the sound of *-ed* is /id/ (*planted; ended*).

DECODING

When decoding words with the suffix *-ed*:
    1. Write and prove the base word.
    2. Rewrite the word with the suffix. (Check for two consonants before adding the suffix.)
    3. Underline the suffix.

    stŏp*   stopp<u>ed</u>   prĭnt**   print<u>ed</u>

A. Underline the suffix in each word.

    mixed   buzzed   ended   landed   kissed

B. Prove the base word. Rewrite the word with the suffix *-ed*. Then underline the suffix.
    Example:

1. b e g _____   4. b u z z _____

2. s m e l l _____   5. s t e p _____

3. s t r e s s _____   6. a s k _____

READING

Read the phone message. Notice the words with the suffix *-ed*.

RETURNED YOUR CALL	WANTS TO SEE YOU

MESSAGE *Hi Julie, it's Jan.*
I called to tell you about Meg's date! I helped her get her hair fixed. She look so cute all dressed up. But I must tell you how the date ended! They stopped out front, walked to the door, and her date hugged her. He got so flustered that he tripped and twisted his ankle! All in all, Meg loved the evening. Call me for more details!

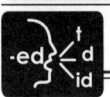

Three Sounds of -ED

APPLICATION ACTIVITIES

A. Circle the final consonant. Write the voiceless symbol (⊖) in the blank if the circled letter is voiceless. Write the voiced symbol (ᗯ) in the blank if the circled letter is voiced.

Example: dro(p) ⊖

1. call ____
2. hug ____
3. stop ____
4. fix ____
5. help ____
6. trip ____
7. dress ____
8. bag ____
9. slam ____

B. Write the words under the correct column. If the suffix -ed is pronounced like the voiceless /t/, write the word under the "/t/ (⊖)" column. If the suffix -ed is pronounced like the voiced /d/, write the word under the "/d/ (ᗯ)" column. If the suffix -ed is pronounced /id/, write the word in the "/id/" column. (Letters betwwn slash marks "/ /" represent sounds.)

added	dropped	fitted	hugged	pulled
bagged	ended	fixed	jumped	stopped
buzzed	filmed	frosted	kissed	tested

/t/ (⊖)	/d/ (ᗯ)	/id/
		added

Student Workbook — Most Common Words List 7

MCW 7

Skills Review
- Most Common Words are words that are used often when reading and sometimes do not follow phonetic skills.

Most Common Words List 7

who	much	think	only	two	its	our
here	over	also	walk	back	other	after

A. Read the story. Circle the Most Common Words from List 7.

I love to visit my grandma. She is getting old, but I think she is still so much fun. She is the only person who can make me feel so good. After school, I walk over to her house. When I get there, she says, "Come here and give me a hug!"

Our favorite thing to do is to play games together. We can play for two hours and not get tired. We also like to do other things like look at her big tree and pick fruit off its branches.

When I leave grandma's house, I already can't wait to go back!

B. Write the missing letters to complete the Most Common Words.

1. t __ __
2. m __ __ h
3. h __ r __
4. __ n __ y
5. w __ __
6. __ a __ k
7. __ __ r
8. __ __ i n k
9. o __ __ r
10. o __ __ e r
11. __ f __ e r
12. i __ __
13. a __ s __
14. w __ __ k

Most Common Words List 7

C. Circle the hidden Most Common Word to complete each sentence. Use the sentence as a clue. Then write the word on the line.

Example: naqg**who**stli (_who_ are you?)

1. thinkchlexu (I _____ she is so fun.)

2. mipgmuchlpw (We have so _____ fun.)

3. tiwhofmoel (She is the one _____ can make me feel good.)

4. tredsconlyj (She is the _____ one.)

5. jafterkgoerl (I go there _____ school.)

6. bwalkxapret (I _____ over to her house after school!)

7. overpeikawl (I go _____ to her house.)

8. matghereciu (Come _____!)

9. twobkempl (We play games for _____ hours.)

10. pertengits (We pick fruit off _____ branches.)

11. nabourlemk (That is _____ favorite thing to do.)

12. efrialsotha (We _____ like to do other things.)

13. rbackstidef (I can't wait to go _____!)

14. decralothert (I like _____ things.)

Student **Workbook**   Name

Lesson 30

Phonetic Skill 3

Skills Review
- When the vowel stands alone (or has no guardian), the vowel sound is *long*.
- Exceptions to this rule: *to*, *the*, *do*, *who*, *two*. (These exception words are taught in the Most Common Words lessons.)

DECODING

To prove the vowel sound in a Phonetic Skill 3 word:
  1. Go under the word left to right. Place an *x* under the vowel.
  2. There are no guardian consonants. Move up and over the vowel.
  3. The vowel stands alone in the word, so mark the vowel long with the long vowel mark (—).

gō̄   hī̄
 x   x

A. Prove the words.

we   me   so   I   be   no

READING

Read these sentences. Notice the Phonetic Skill 3 words.

I must get a gift for my mom. Jo will help me. We will go to the mall. It will be good to have her help. I am so glad she did not say no.

APPLICATION ACTIVITIES

A. List four words that follow Phonetic Skill 3 from the sentences above.

1. _____
2. _____
3. _____
4. _____

Lesson 30 Name *Student* **Workbook**

Phonetic Skill 3

B. Read each word. Is the vowel short or long? Write the word in the correct column and prove the word.

| ~~he~~ | hit | go | help | got | hi |

       ŭ   ─

_____   *hē* / x

_____   _____

_____   _____

C. Write each word under the picture it rhymes with. More than one word matches the same picture.

| ~~we~~ | so | hi | go | I |
| he | me | no | be | |

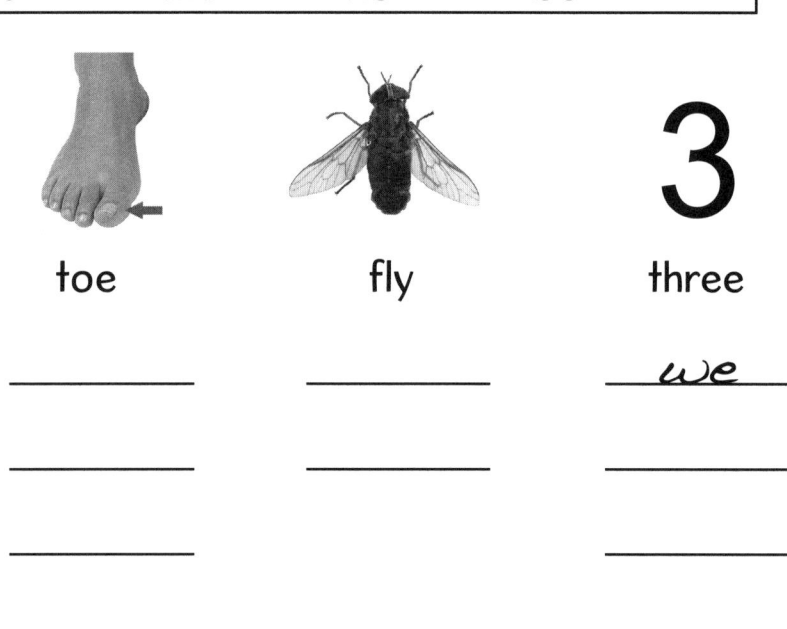

toe   fly   three

_____   _____   *we*

_____   _____   _____

_____   _____   _____

                          _____

Student **Workbook**   Name

Lesson 31

Phonetic Skill 4

Skills Review
- When the vowel e comes at the end of a word, the e is *silent*, making the first vowel sound *long*.
- The consonant between the first vowel and silent e cannot act as a guardian consonant because the e makes the first vowel sound long.

DECODING

To prove the vowel sound in a Phonetic Skill 4 word:
1. Move *under* the word, moving left to right. Place an x under the first vowel and under the vowel e.
2. Move up and over the e. Draw a line straight down through the vowel e and the x below it, making it silent.
3. Move left across the consonant to the first vowel.
4. The e causes the first vowel sound to be long, so mark the vowel long.

A. (Circle) the words that have a long vowel sound.

(state)   can   side   life   man   same

late   plan   vote   take   red   sun

B. Prove these words.

cute   safe   make   time

drive   rule   home   name

READING

Read the ad. Notice the Phonetic Skill 4 words.

Jane's *Travel* Co.

Do you want to go on a fun trip but don't want to spend a lot of time and money to plan it?

We'll help you plan your trip for a great price!

On your trip, you'll:
- Take a nice plane flight.
- Stay in a cute home on the lake.
- Go on a nine mile bike ride around the lake.
- Enjoy fine dining at night.
- Go on a drive to a cave.

You'll like your trip so much that you'll hate to go home!

Lesson 31   Name   Student **Workbook**

 Phonetic Skill 4

APPLICATION ACTIVITIES

A. Add a silent *e* to each word to make a new word.
Example: **cap**   **cape**

1. quit _____   5. cub _____

2. tap   _____   6. not _____

3. cod   _____   7. hat _____

4. tub   _____   8. rip _____

B. Write the correct word by adding a silent *e* to the end of the word in parentheses.
Example: If you want to go on a trip, call <u>Jane</u>. (Jan)

1. We'll choose the best _____ for your trip! **(sit)**

2. Enjoy every _____ of your meals! **(bit)**

3. Go on a trip _____ for you! **(mad)**

4. Get the best _____ in town! **(rat)**

5. You'll like your trip so much that you'll _____ to go again next year! **(hop)**

C. Find and circle the silent *e* words in the word search. Words can go down ↓, across →, or diagonal ↘↗.

s	a	l	e	e	u	o
s	m	i	l	e	o	c
s	t	o	v	e	e	q
i	h	q	k	e	d	g
z	l	i	n	e	a	a
e	r	u	d	e	t	m
t	t	w	a	v	e	e

date   line   size
stove   game   rude
smile   tune   hole
sale   smoke   wave

80   ReadingHorizons®

Student **Workbook**   Name

Lesson 32
Another Sound for *C* and *G*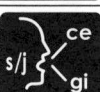

Skills Review

- When *c* is followed by an *i* or an *e*, it will change its sound from /k/ to /s/.
- When *g* is followed by an *i* or an *e*, it will sometimes change its sound from /g/ to /j/.
- When *two* consonants come between the first vowel and the silent *e*, the *two* consonants will act as *guardians*, making the first vowel short (*dance*, *prince*, *plunge*). Exceptions: *-ange* (*strange*); *-aste* (*paste*).
- English words never end in the letter *j*. When the sound /j/ is heard at the end of a word, it will always be spelled *-ge*. Words with a long vowel sound will end with the *-ge* spelling (*cage*). Words with a short vowel sound will end with *-dge* spelling (*judge*; *bridge*).

DECODING

- Draw an arc above the *ci* or *ce*, and write an *s* above the arc. This is called a *bridge s*.

- Draw an arc above the *gi* or *ge*, and write a *j* above the arc. This is called a *bridge j*.

   bridge

1. Mark the bridge *s* and bridge *j* in these words.

wage   place   gel   prince

2. Prove these words.

age   cell   stage   since

ice   gem   face   judge

READING

Read the posters. Notice the bridge *s* and bridge *j* words.

Lesson 32 — Name _____   Student **Workbook**

 **Another Sound for *C* and *G***

APPLICATION ACTIVITIES

A. Unscramble the phrases and sentences from the poster on the previous page. Write them on the lines below.

1. dice! / Roll / the _____

2. a / day! / Twice _____

3. rides! / Space / age _____

4. for / price! / See / low / a _____

B. Create words by adding letters to the words below. Use the letters or Blends listed in the box. Add the letter(s) to the first of the word.

n sp w r s tw br f m pr pl tr c st p

Example: **-ice: <u>mice</u>**

1. **-ice:** ___ice   ___ice   ___ice   ___ice

2. **-ace:** ___ace   ___ace   ___ace   ___ace

3. **-age:** ___age   ___age   ___age   ___age

C. Read each word. Decide how the *c* and *g* in each word are pronounced. Write the words in the correct columns.

~~case~~   deck   gin   huge
~~cent~~   face   gist   lace
cite   game   gum   lodge

/k/	/s/	/g/	/j/
case	cent		

82

Student **Workbook**   Name   Lesson 33

Adding Suffixes to Phonetic Skills 3 and 4

Skills Review

Adding Suffixes to Phonetic Skill 3 Words
- To add the suffixes -ing, -ed, -er, and -est to Phonetic Skill 3 words, just add the suffix (go/go<u>ing</u>).

Adding Suffixes to Phonetic Skill 4 Words
- When adding the suffixes -ing, -ed, -er, and -est to Phonetic Skill 4 words, drop the e, and add the suffix (ride/rid<u>ing</u>; dance/danc<u>ing</u>).
- When adding suffixes to words ending in silent e that do not begin in e or i, such as -able, -ness, -ful, and -less, the e is *not* dropped from the base word. The silent e remains with the word when the suffix is added (hope/hope<u>ful</u>).

DECODING

To prove words with suffixes:
1. Prove the base word.
2. Rewrite the word with the suffix.
3. Underline the suffix.

     gō   go<u>ing</u>   hōpe̸   hop<u>ing</u>

A. Underline the suffix in each word.

     ageless   liked   hopeful   smiling

B. Prove the base word. Rewrite the word with the suffix. Then underline the suffix.

     Example: jōke̸ (-ing) jok<u>ing</u>

1. b e (-ing) _____
2. s a v e (-ed) _____
3. g r a c e (-ful) _____
4. l i k e (-ness) _____
5. n i c e (-er) _____
6. l a t e (-est) _____
7. h o p e (-less) _____
8. d r i v e (-able) _____

READING

Read these sentences. Notice the Phonetic Skill 3 and 4 words that have suffixes.

I've been driving around for the past hour, thinking about the cutest girl in my class. I think I'm going to ask her to a dance. I'm not the bravest person when it comes to dating or dancing, but I am hopeful!

ReadingHorizons®

Lesson 33 — Name — Student **Workbook**

Adding Suffixes to Phonetic Skills 3 and 4

APPLICATION ACTIVITIES

A. Change the words from the sentences on the previous page to new words. First, write the base word. Then rewrite the word with the suffix.
Example: **driving – ing =** <u>drive</u> **+ er =** <u>driver</u>

1. cutest – est = _____ + er = _____

2. dating – ing = _____ + ed = _____

3. hopeful – ful = _____ + less = _____

4. dancing – ing = _____ + er = _____

B. Write the base word for each word that has a suffix.
Example: hiding   hide

Word with Suffix: Base Word: Word with Suffix: Base Word:

1. <u>cuter</u>   _____   4. <u>finest</u>   _____

2. <u>riding</u>   _____   5. <u>prideful</u> _____

3. <u>voted</u>   _____   6. <u>timeless</u> _____

C. Complete the crossword puzzle.

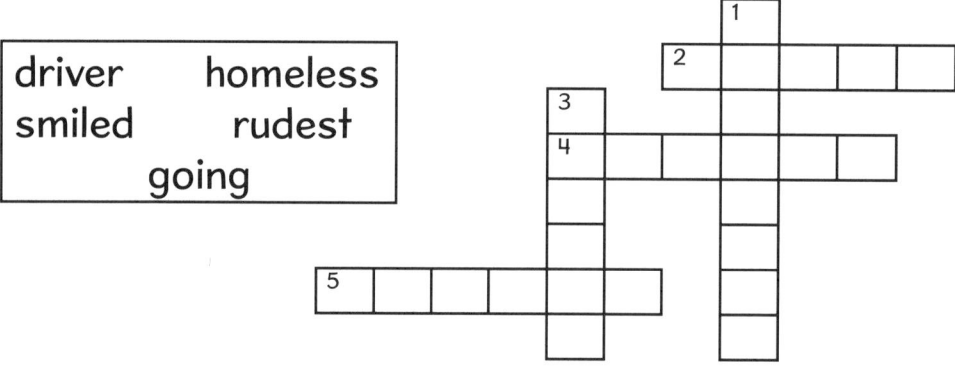

driver   homeless
smiled   rudest
      going

Across
2. Moving from one place to another (I am _____ shopping after work.)
4. The most rude (He was the _____ person I've ever talked to.)
5. Past tense of smile (The baby _____ at me when I looked at her.)

Down
1. Without a home (There are many people who are _____ who sleep in the park at night.)
3. A person who guides a car or bus (I am a good _____; I've never gotten a speeding ticket.)

Student Workbook   Name

Lesson 34

Sounds of *GH*, *IGH*, and *IGHT*

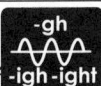

Skills Review

The combination *gh* can do three things:
1) When *gh* comes at the beginning of a word, it has the sound /g/ (*ghost*).
2) When *gh* comes at the end of a word, it sometimes has the sound /f/ (*laugh*).
3) In most words, the *gh* is silent. When the vowel *i* comes before the *gh*, the *i* is long, and the *gh* is silent (*high*; *night*).

DECODING

When *gh* is at the beginning of a word, mark the *h* silent.

gh̸ost

When *gh* is at the end of a word and it says /f/, mark a small *f* above the *gh*.

laugh (with *f* above *gh*)

When *gh* is in the combination *igh*, cross out the *g* and the *h*, and mark the *i* long.

rīg̸h̸t

A. Prove these words. The *gh* is silent.

bright	high	night	tight
sigh	fight	light	flight

READING

Read the signs. Notice the words that contain *gh*, *igh*, and *ight*.

Sounds of *GH*, *IGH*, and *IGHT*

APPLICATION ACTIVITIES

A. Unscramble the letters to make words using *gh*, *igh*, and *ight*. The words are used in the signs on the previous page.

1. gtnih _____

2. ghih _____

3. rugoh _____

4. sthog _____

5. sthgi _____

6. gouht _____

B. Circle the words in which *gh* is silent. Underline the word in which *gh* says /g/. Draw a box around the words in which *gh* says /f/. The first one is done for you.

light   ghost   tough   might   right

flight   high   rough   plight   laugh

night   fight   bright   sight   cough

C. Write a meaningful sentence using one word from Activity B. Try to use at least seven words in your sentence.

_____

_____

Student Workbook   Name   Lesson 35

Phonetic Skill 5 and Adjacent Vowels

Skills Review
- When vowels stand next to each other, they are adjacent.
- When vowels are adjacent, the second vowel is silent, and the first vowel sound is long.
- These are the adjacent vowels: *ai ay ea ee oa oe ui ue ie*

DECODING

To prove the vowel sound in a Phonetic Skill 5 word:
1. Move *under* the word, left to right. Place an *x* under each vowel.
2. Continue moving to the right until you reach the end of the word, and then move up and left to the vowel. Mark the vowel silent by drawing a line straight down through the vowel and the *x* underneath.
3. Move left to the next vowel, and mark it long.

see   wait

A. Circle the Phonetic Skill 5 words.

vote   (feel)   true   like   paint   street

keep   line   least   road   read   hope

B. Prove these words.

need   heat   rain   say   pie

blue   boat   toe   lie   fruit

C. Write the Phonetic Skill 5 words from Activity B under the correct vowel sound. The first one is done.

ā	ē	ō	ū	ī
	need			

READING

Read the menu. Notice the Phonetic Skill 5 words.

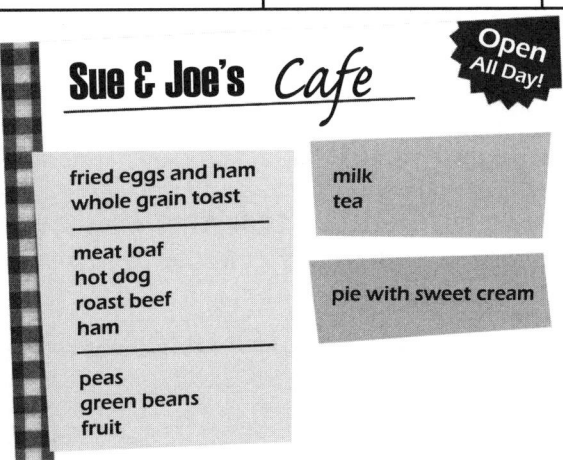

Sue & Joe's Cafe — Open All Day!

fried eggs and ham
whole grain toast

milk
tea

meat loaf
hot dog
roast beef
ham

pie with sweet cream

peas
green beans
fruit

Phonetic Skill 5 and Adjacent Vowels

APPLICATION ACTIVITIES

A. Write the words from the box next to the word it rhymes with.
   Example: **cream** _stream_

   | toast   train   pea   green   beat   leaf |

   1. roast _____   4. bean _____

   2. tea _____   5. sweet _____

   3. beef _____   6. grain _____

B. Change the adjacent vowels to make a new word.
   Example: **say: ay → ee** _see_

   1. **due:** ue → ie = _____   4. **lead:** ea → oa = _____

   2. **mail:** ai → ea = _____   5. **toe:** oe → ea = _____

   3. **seat:** ea → ui = _____   6. **soak:** oa → ee = _____

C. Fill in the missing vowels to complete the adjacent vowel patterns.

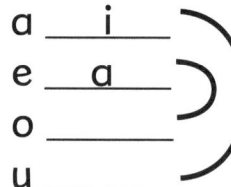
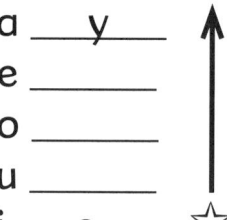

D. Choose your favorite meal from the menu on the previous page. Write what menu item you would choose in complete sentences on the lines below. Try to use commas in your sentences.

_____

_____

Student Workbook   Name ___   Lesson 36

Adding Suffixes to Phonetic Skill 5

Skills Review
- To add the suffixes *-ing*, *-ed*, *-er*, and *-est* to Phonetic Skill 5 words, just add the suffix.

DECODING

To prove words with suffixes:
1. Prove the base word.
2. Rewrite the word with the suffix.
3. Underline the suffix.

nēed   need<u>ed</u>   wāit   wait<u>ing</u>

A. Underline the suffix in each word.

keeping   meanest   painted   weaker

B. Prove the base word. Rewrite the word with the suffix. Then underline the suffix.

Example: wāit (-ed) wait<u>ed</u>

1. clean (-er) _____   4. rain (-ing) _____

2. deep (-est) _____   5. claim (-ed) _____

3. fail (-ed) _____   6. heat (-ing) _____

READING

Read this restaurant ad. Notice the Phonetic Skill 5 words that have suffixes.

---

the Steakhouse

Try our roasted meat with rice and toasted nuts.

Voted cleanest eating place.

You will be seated right away. No waiting.

Lesson 36 — Name _____ *Student Workbook*

Adding Suffixes to Phonetic Skill 5

APPLICATION ACTIVITIES

A. Complete the restaurant ad with the correct words from the box.

| seated | roasted | cleanest | toasted | waiting |

Try our _____ meat with rice and _____ nuts.
              a.   b.

Voted _____ eating place.
            c.

You will be _____ right away. No _____!
              d.   e.

B. Choose the correct word to complete each sentence.

1. It's 10:00 a.m. and Jim is still _____! Should I go wake him up? (sleeper/sleeping)
2. I think I've _____ 10 pounds from eating so many treats over the holidays. (gained/gaining)
3. I _____ my friend's letter when I went to the post office. (mailed/mailing)
4. I _____ my white shirt when I spilled grape juice on it. (stained/staining)
5. I got a ticket for _____. I didn't know the speed limit was only 25 miles per hour. (speeder/speeding)

C. Read each ad. Write the base word of the underlined word.
Example: No <u>waiting</u>!   <u>wait</u>

1. <u>Seeking</u> a job? Call 555-1111. _____
2. Want <u>greener</u> grass? Call the Grass Hoppers! _____
3. Street <u>sweeping</u> daily at 5:00 a.m. _____
4. Need a home loan? <u>Loaning</u> to first-time home buyers. _____
5. Get a job worth <u>boasting</u> about! Call today! _____

Student *Workbook*   Name

Most Common Words List 8

Skills Review
- Most Common Words are words that are used often when reading and sometimes do not follow phonetic skills.

Most Common Words List 8

boy	use	three	before	new	work	first
may	way	again	ever	never	seven	want

A. Read the story. Circle the Most Common Words from List 8. Some words are used more than once.

Every day, I wake up at 6:00 a.m. First, I run three laps around the block. I want to stay fit! Then I get ready for work.

Before I go to work, I read the paper to see what is new. On my way to work, I drop my seven-year-old boy off at school.

If I feel tired, I may stop for a cup of tea. I use it to stay awake at work. But I never drink tea before I go to bed. One time when I did that, I couldn't sleep all night. I don't want to do that ever again!

B. One of the words in each set is a Most Common Word, and the other is a nonsense word. Circle the Most Common Word.

Example: (boy)   bou

1. use   ase
2. bifare   before
3. first   frist
4. evar   ever
5. seven   svnee
6. yob   boy
7. way   awy

8. wnta   want
9. navre   never
10. yma   may
11. new   enw
12. rethe   three
13. work   wrko
14. again   agien

Most Common Words List 8

C. Choose the correct Most Common Word to complete the sentence, and write it in the blank.

1. That __boy__ is 11 years old. (boy/before)

2. I _____ the rag to clean. (never/use)

3. I have _____ kids. (three/ever)

4. I go running _____ I go to work. (before/again)

5. I don't want to do that _____. (again/never)

6. I got a _____ car! (never/new)

7. I go to _____ at 7:00 a.m. (three/work)

8. I don't _____ want to do that again! (seven/ever)

9. The _____ thing I do when I wake up is go running. (first/may)

10. I _____ stop for a bite to eat. (may/boy)

11. I drop my boy off on my _____ to work. (want/way)

12. My boy is _____ years old. (seven/before)

13. I _____ want to do that again! (never/new)

14. I _____ to stay fit, so I go running. (way/want)

Student Workbook   Name

Chapter 3
Reading in Context

Practice reading this advertisement using all the skills you've learned in Chapter 3. Review the words that are difficult for you. Then read the advertisement to a teacher or friend.

Spending too much on rent?
Scrimping and saving to get a home?
Get your dream home now!

Home Loans

The first 10 people who come in will get a free set of gold clubs!

RATES FROM 5.7%

Times are tough now. Many people are thinking, "Is it the right time to get a home?" Well...

Prices are coming down.
Rates are coming down.
Find the right home, and then you come on down.

Bank of the East *A hand held.*

We tell you about all fees and taxes before you take out a loan. You will save with Bank of the East.

Reading in Context

Practice reading this article using all the skills you've learned in Chapter 3. Review the words that are difficult for you. Then read the article to a teacher or friend.

BIG WIN FOR WEST HIGH

Last night West High pulled off a big win over East High, beating them 78 to 65. West led with Steve Gill's dunking and Ben Hall's speed. Hall kept the game at a fast pace. West's passing game was strong. East's was like dodge ball. Late in the game, Gill had a bad fall and went out with a sprain. With Gill out, East gained a slight lead, but they could not hold it.

With this win, West will go on to their last game. Two weeks from now, they will face Lone Peak High. Before then, the team will have time to rest. West is hopeful that Gill will heal. They are going to need him.

Student Workbook Name _____   Lesson 37

Contractions

Skills Review
- Contractions are words that have been reduced by leaving some letters out.
- An apostrophe (') is used in the exact place where letters have been left out. Example: *Let us* is rewritten as *let's*.

LIST OF COMMON CONTRACTIONS

NOT		**HAVE**		**WILL**	
are not	aren't	could have	could've	he will	he'll
cannot	can't	I have	I've	it will	it'll
could not	couldn't	should have	should've	I will	I'll
did not	didn't	they have	they've	she will	she'll
do not	don't	we have	we've	they will	they'll
does not	doesn't	you have	you've	we will	we'll
has not	hasn't	who have	who've	who will	who'll
have not	haven't			you will	you'll
is not	isn't	**IS**			
should not	shouldn't	he is	he's	**HAD**	
was not	wasn't	here is	here's	he had	he'd
were not	weren't	it is	it's	I had	I'd
will not	won't	she is	she's	she had	she'd
		that is	that's	they had	they'd
WOULD		there is	there's	we had	we'd
he would	he'd	what is	what's	you had	you'd
I would	I'd	who is	who's		
she would	she'd			**ARE**	
we would	we'd	**US**		they are	they're
who would	who'd	let us	let's	we are	we're
you would	you'd			you are	you're
		AM			
		I am	I'm		

APPLICATION ACTIVITIES

A. Write the contractions for the following words

1. have not _haven't_
2. she would _____
3. they are _____
4. she is _____
5. we had _____
6. let us _____
7. we will _____
8. who have _____
9. I am _____
10. will not _____

Contractions

B. Draw a line from the word on the left to the contraction on the right.

1. cannot — I'll
2. there is — can't
3. we are — that's
4. you would — wasn't
5. we had — there's
6. should have — you're
7. you are — you'd
8. was not — should've
9. that is — we're
10. I will — we'd

C. Use the contractions in Activity B to finish the sentences. Not all of them will be used.

1. The boy _____ finished his jobs before he went outside to play.

2. _____ go to the play if you want me to go.

3. It _____ a good idea to feed the dog fruit.

4. _____ the best football player I know.

5. I _____ go to school today. I'm sick.

Student **Workbook**   Name

Lesson 38

Many Jobs of Y

Skills Review
- The letter *y* has more than one sound.
- *Y* at the beginning of a word is a *consonant*.
- *Y* anywhere else in a word is a *vowel*. If *y* is the only working (sounded) vowel in the word, it will have the sound of *i*. Place a small *i* above the *y*. Use the Five Phonetic Skills to determine if *y* has the sound of short *i* or long *i*. *Y* can also be a silent adjacent vowel (*key*; *pay*)
- *Y* in bridge *s* and bridge *j* words: When *y* is next to *c* or *g* in a word, it creates the same sound as *ci* and *gi* (*cyst*; *gym*).

DECODING

Decode words using the Five Phonetic Skills.

Prove these words.

Job 1: *Y* can be a consonant.

yet   yes   yoke   yeast

Job 2: *Y* can have the sound of short *i* when it follows Phonetic Skills 1 and 2.

pyx   crypt   Syd   Lynn

Job 3: *Y* can have the sound of long *i* when it follows Phonetic Skills 3 and 4.

my   try   style   bye

Job 4: *Y* is silent when it is an adjacent vowel.

say   key   way   stay

READING

Read the story. Notice the words with *y*.

"Lynn!" Lyle yelled from across the street. "Want to play?"

Lynn groaned and rolled over on the grass. What should she say? She just wanted to lay here in the yard all day and read. This book was just her type. It was written in a style she liked. The hero had just found the key to a stolen treasure hidden in a crypt!

"Yes, I'll play," Lynn yelled back, "but not yet. Let me try to finish my book first."

Many Jobs of Y

APPLICATION ACTIVITIES

A. Circle the word that rhymes with the word from the story on the previous page.

1. **Lynn:**   twist   spin   can   fake

2. **play:**   plop   cape   tray   wait

3. **my:**   hi   may   mop   yam

4. **type:**   kite   tape   tin   wipe

B. Unscramble each word from the story. Write it in the blank to complete the sentence.

1. lledey _____
   a.

   "Lynn!" Lyle _____ from across the street.
                     b.

2. yad _____
   a.

   She just wanted to lay here in the yard all _____ and read.
                                                                          b.

3. ylste _____
   a.

   It was written in a _____ she liked.
                             b.

4. pcyrt _____
   a.

   The hero had just found the key to a stolen treasure hidden in the _____.
                                               b.

C. Prove the words. Circle the words in which y is making the short i sound. Underline the words in which y is making the long i sound. Put a box around the words in which y is silent. Note: You should have two words left. They are words in which y is a consonant.

[boxed] grāy   [circled] crӯpt   [underlined] drȳ   yum

gym   may   cry   pay

cyst   sky   yell   type

Student **Workbook**   Name

Lesson 39

Decoding Skill 1

Skills Review

Decoding words with more than one working (or sounded) vowel:
- If there is just *one* guardian consonant following the vowel in a multi-syllabic word, the consonant will move on to be with the vowel in the next syllable. "*One* must run."
- You do not need to mark guardian consonants in multi-syllabic words.

DECODING

1. Mark under the word, left to right, marking each vowel with an *x*. Be sure to arc blends when you see them.

   motel
   x   x

2. Go back to the first vowel.

   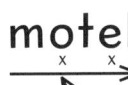

3. Only one guardian consonant, the letter *t*, follows the vowel *o*, so it goes on to the next syllable. Box the first syllable after the vowel. The *o* is long because it stands alone in the first syllable, so mark the vowel *o* long.

4. The vowel in the second syllable is short because it still has a guardian. Mark the vowel *e* short, and box the final syllable. We do not need to mark guardians with a star in multi-syllabic words.

   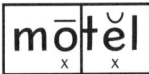

A. Prove these words.

robot   begin   provide   decide

delay   behave   nomad   refrain

READING

Read the article. Notice the Decoding Skill 1 words.

NEWS FLASH

Recently, a crisis at Fremont College has taken place. Students protest that the demands placed on them to gain a degree are too high. When asked to refrain from continuing their protest, they recite, "We will proceed to protect our rights."

Reading*Horizons*®   99

Lesson 39 Name Student **Workbook**

Decoding Skill 1

APPLICATION ACTIVITIES

A. Match the first syllable on the left with the correct second syllable on the right to make a word.

1. pro		max
2. cli		have
3. re		sis
4. de		test
5. cri		cite
6. be		gree

(Line drawn from "pro" to "test")

B. Write each word from Activity A on the lines below.

1. _____   4. _____
2. _____   5. _____
3. _____   6. _____

C. The words have been divided incorrectly. Put the syllable line in the correct place to make your syllable boxes. Then prove the word.

Example: proc|eed   prō|ceed

Incorrect: Correct:

1. don|ate   donate
2. prog|ram   program
3. recli|ne   recline
4. dem|and   demand
5. dig|est   digest

D. Use two of the words from Activity C above to complete the paragraph.

The recent crisis at Fremont has to do with the _____ placed on the students to gain a degree. I went to that college and have been asked to _____ money. In light of this, I don't think I will.

Student Workbook Name **Lesson 40**

Syllable Stress and the Schwa

Skills Review
- Every word of more than one syllable has one syllable that is emphasized more than the other(s).
- *Stress* is the amount of volume and pitch given to a sound, syllable, or word when saying a multi-syllabic word.
- Stressed sounds, syllables, and words are pronounced louder and longer than unstressed ones.
- Unstressed syllables often assume the schwa sound. The schwa is the *unstressed* vowel sound or syllable in a multi-syllabic word. It is represented by an upside-down e (ə). The sound of the schwa is the short *u* (*about*) and sometimes short *i* (*leverage*).
- The vowel *a* is often associated with the schwa sound as a word in a sentence (*I saw a cat*) or in the spelling at the beginning or end of a word (*agenda*).
- All vowels can take the schwa sound.

DECODING

Prove the word according to the phonetic and decoding skills. If the vowel sound takes on the schwa sound, you can put the schwa (ə) above the vowel. (Note: You can use either lines or boxes to divide syllables.)

A. Prove the words. Write the schwa mark above the vowel in the unstressed syllable.

sofa   pencil   human   even

student   local   moment   agree

B. Which syllable has the stronger stress? Prove the words. Then circle the syllable that has the stronger stress.

Example: nĕglĕct

silent   select   divide   label

APPLICATION ACTIVITIES

A. Complete each sentence with the correct word from the box.

ago	equal	private	adult
evil	adopt	legal	final

1. When I turn 18, I will be an _____.

2. Many stories contain a theme about good versus _____.

3. It is not _____ for me to drive until I am 16 years old.

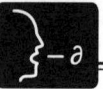

Syllable Stress and the Schwa

4. My grandfather was born a long time _____.

5. To be fair to both of us, we should cut the last piece of pie into two slices of _____ size.

6. I don't go to a public school; I go to a _____ one.

7. My uncle and aunt want a child, so they are going to try to _____ a baby from China.

8. I have a _____ exam next week, so I need to study for the test.

B. Decide which syllable has the stronger stress. Use the words from the sentences in Activity A. If the word has the stronger stress in the first syllable, write it in the column on the left ("1st Syllable"). If the word has the stronger stress in the second syllable, write it in the column on the right ("2nd Syllable").

~~ago~~   equal   private   adult

evil   adopt   legal   final

1st Syllable	2nd Syllable
	ago

Student Workbook   Name   Lesson 41

Last Job of Y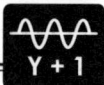

Skills Review
- When *y* comes at the end of a word and there is another working vowel that comes before it in the word, the *y* will take the sound of long *e* (lad*y*; dail*y*; bab*y*).
- Exception: When *y* comes at the end of a word and *n*, *f*, or *l* comes before it, and the word is a verb, the *y* will say long *i* (den*y*; def*y*; rel*y*).
- When *y* comes in the first syllable of a multi-syllabic word and stands alone, the *y* will take the long *i* sound (c*y*clone, C*y*prus, T*y*son).

DECODING

Mark the word according the phonetic and decoding skills. Place an *e* or *i* above the *y*, and mark it long.

baby   lazy

deny   cyclone

A. Prove these words in which *y* ends in the sound of long *e*.

tiny   crazy   lady   navy

rainy   tidy   holy   greedy

B. Prove these words in which *y* ends in the sound of long *i*.

reply   rely   deny   defy

C. Prove these words in which *y* comes in the first syllable and has the sound of long *i*.

Cyprus   Tyson   cyclone

READING

Read the story. Notice the two-syllable words with *y*.

It was a lazy summer day. I sat in the park and watched a lady take her tiny baby for a pony ride. "Be careful!" I kept thinking. I cannot deny that it made me uneasy to watch, though I don't mean to imply that the lady was not a good mother.

Lesson 41 Name

Last Job of Y

APPLICATION ACTIVITIES

A. Answer the questions about the story on the previous page with the correct word that follows the Last Job of Y.

1. What type of summer day was it? _____

2. What type of ride did the baby go on? _____

3. Who took the baby for a ride? _____

B. Find and circle these words that follow the Last Job of Y in the word search. Words can go down ↓, across →, or diagonal ↘ ↗.

h	r	v	r	i	j	g	m	q	q
k	o	v	b	o	n	y	h	r	z
m	f	l	y	r	c	r	a	z	y
d	k	n	y	z	q	z	z	k	t
o	o	s	l	a	z	y	y	j	i
p	h	g	q	j	z	b	r	m	n
t	i	d	y	i	d	a	n	g	y
d	b	a	b	y	b	r	a	e	e
x	j	l	m	n	n	t	v	g	h
i	c	y	r	a	i	n	y	o	x

baby	hazy	lazy	rainy
bony	holy	navy	tidy
crazy	icy	pony	tiny

Student **Workbook** Name Lesson 42

Decoding Skill 2

Skills Review

Decoding words with more than one working (or sounded) vowel:
- If there are *two* guardian consonants following a vowel in a multi-syllabic word (and the consonants are not a Blend), the consonants will split. One consonant will stay with the first vowel, and the other consonant will move on to be with the vowel in the next syllable. "*Two* must split."
- You do not need to mark guardian consonants in multi-syllabic words.

DECODING

1. Mark under the word, left to right, marking each vowel with an *x*. Be sure to arc Blends when you see them.

    c a m p u s
      x   x

2. Go back to the first vowel.

    c a m p u s
      x   x

3. Two guardian consonants follow the vowel *a*, so they will split. Box the first syllable between the two consonants. The *a* is short because it still has a guardian, so mark the vowel *a* short.

    | c ă m | p u s
       x   x

4. The vowel in the second syllable is also short because it still has a guardian. Mark the vowel *u* short, and box the final syllable. Remember that we do not need to mark guardians with a star.

    | c ă m | p ŭ s |
       x   x

A. Prove these words.

explain   candy   sixteen   dictate

maintain   invite   subject   engage

READING

Read the letter. Notice the Decoding Skill 2 words.

Dear Mr. Jensen:

I was not happy with my stay at your motel on Sunday, June 16. I want to explain why I am upset.

When I first got to the motel, the man at the front desk made me wait fifteen minutes before he spoke to me. When I finally got to my room, it was very unclean. There was fungus in the tub and dandruff on the pillow. The strong smell of smoke made it difficult to inhale. Also, the console table was broken. When I tried to use the coffee maker, it began to make funny sounds, and then it looked like it was going to explode! Indeed, I wanted to go on a rampage, except I was too sleepy!

I would like to request a refund. Please call me to discuss this in more detail.

Sincerely,

Betty Updike

Lesson 42 — Decoding Skill 2

APPLICATION ACTIVITIES

A. Write the correct second syllable in the blank to make a word. The words are found in the reading activity on the previous page.

1. fif _teen_ :   -deed   -clude   -teen   -cline
2. up _____ :   -vade   -set   -plete   -tein
3. in _____ :   -hale   -dom   -grene   -tence
4. con _____ :   -nis   -tail   -made   -sole
5. ex _____ :   -tal   -plode   -vide   -dred

B. The words have been divided incorrectly. Put the syllable line in the correct place to make your syllable boxes. Then prove the word.

Example: ex c|e p t   [ĕx|cēpt]

Incorrect: Correct:

1. u p s|e t   u p s e t
2. a b s|e n t   a b s e n t
3. e x p|e c t   e x p e c t
4. i n c|l u d e   i n c l u d e
5. c o m p|l a i n c o m p l a i n

C. Use three words from Activity B above to complete the paragraph.

The main reason for the letter to Mr. Jensen was to _____(1)_____ about the service. Writing the letter helped Betty explain why she was _____(2)_____. It was important that she _____(3)_____ all the reasons so that Mr. Jensen understood.

Student Workbook Name _____

Lesson 43

Prefixes

Skills Review
- A prefix is one or more letters added to the *beginning* of a word that changes the meaning of the word. Examples: *Jan is <u>un</u>happy. Please <u>re</u>state your name.*

DECODING

When decoding a word with a prefix, first underline the prefix. Then decode the rest of the word.

List of Common Prefixes

un-	(opposite)	over-	(excessive)	trans-	(across)
re-	(again)	mis-	(bad; incorrect)	super-	(above)
in-, im-, il-, ir-	(not)	sub-	(below)	semi-	(half)
dis-	(not)	pre-	(before)	anti-	(opposite)
en-, em-	(put into)	inter-	(between)	mid-	(middle)
non-	(not)	fore-	(earlier)	under-	(too little)
in-, im-	(in)	de-	(reverse)		

A. Prove these words.

untie   refill   predict   dislike

nonstop   invent   overpass   misjudge

APPLICATION ACTIVITIES

A. Match the prefix with the correct base word. Use the sentence as a clue. Write the word in the blank to complete the sentence.

1. **non-:**   life   stop   act   due

   I like _____ flights because I don't like layovers.

2. **re-:**   plant   bend   pay   scribe

   Thank you for your help. How can I ever _____ you?

3. **mid-:**   size   sure   put   lap

   When I rent a car, I always get a _____ car because it's not too big, and it's not too small.

Lesson 43 Name Student **Workbook**

 **Prefixes**

4. **over-**   bug   fit   cast   eat

Even though this food tastes really good, I'm going to try to not _____. I'm trying to watch my weight.

5. **mis-**   ply   side   try   behave

She is a very patient person, especially when her small children _____.

B. Complete each word by adding the correct prefix. Use the definitions in parentheses as clues.

| re | un |

1. ____play (to play again)
2. ____happy (not happy)
3. ____kind (not kind)
4. ____tell (to tell the story again)
5. ____fair (not fair)
6. ____try (to try again)

C. Circle the word with the prefix in each sentence. Then write the prefix on the line below the sentence.

1. I don't drive. I take the (subway).
   Prefix: _____sub_____

2. Even though we disagree on many things, we are still good friends.
   Prefix: _____

3. The students' desks were in the shape of a semicircle so they could all see the teacher.
   Prefix: _____

4. The meat is frozen, so I will defrost it.
   Prefix: _____

5. I'm sorry I'm unable to come to your party. I wish I could!
   Prefix: _____

Student **Workbook**   Name   Lesson 44

-LE at the End of a Word

Skills Review

- Every word or syllable must have a vowel or a vowel sound. In multi-syllabic words, some syllables do not have a working vowel—only a vowel sound. This occurs in words that end in *-le*.
- The *-le* becomes its own syllable at the end of a word. The consonant that comes before the *-le* always stays with the *-le* ending. Sometimes the consonant that precedes the *l* makes an *l*-blend (*simple*; *humble*), and sometimes it does not (*middle*; *little*). Exception: If a word ends in *-ckle*, never separate the *c* and *k*. Divide the syllable *after* the *ck* (*pickle*; *tackle*).
- When a word ends in *-le*, the final vowel *e* is silent, but it creates a new sound for the consonant *l*. A schwa sound comes before the *l* and makes the /ul/ sound (*table*; *eagle*).
- When consonants are doubled before *-le*, do not pronounce the first consonant (*apple*, *bubble*). Even though it is not pronounced, it keeps the first vowel short.

DECODING

If the consonant before the *l* makes an *l*-Blend, then arc them together. Remember the consonant must stay with the *l* to create the vowel sound, so divide in front of the consonant. (Exception: *ck*). Put a schwa mark between the consonant and the *l* to show the vowel sound.

staple   little   tackle

A. Prove these words.

pickle   puzzle   cable   eagle

simple   table   uncle   giggle

APPLICATION ACTIVITIES

cra-	crum-	lit-	bot-	pud-
~~ta-~~	nee-	tum-	sta-	man-

A. Use the syllables listed in the box above, and combine them with the *-le* ending listed to create at least three words.

1. -ble
    words: ___table___, _____, _____
2. -tle
    words: _____, _____, _____
3. -dle
    words: _____, _____, _____

ReadingHorizons®   109

Lesson 44 — -LE at the End of the Word

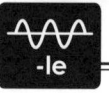

B. Use the correct word to complete the sentence. Write the word in the space provided.

1. The mother put her baby in the _____ to sleep.

    bundle   cradle   bottle   kettle

2. When the lights went out, we lit a _____ so we could see.

    fiddle   candle   staple   tumble

3. The man put the horse in the _____.

    puddle   tumble   stable   puzzle

4. You need a _____ and some thread to sew on a button.

    needle   fable   little   puddle

5. After dinner, everyone in the family played an instrument. I played my _____.

    bundle   cable   fiddle   tumble

Student **Workbook**   Name

Lesson 45

Decode Words of Any Length

Skills Review
- Words of any length can be decoded using both Decoding Skills 1 and 2.

DECODING

Mark everything under the word, working left to right. Go back to the beginning of the word and divide the word into syllables according to Decoding Skills 1 and 2, and prove one syllable at a time.

A. Prove these words.

independence   romantic

equipment   absolute

*tramsomime   concentrate

READING

Read the ads. Notice the multi-syllabic words.

WANT ADS
CONDO FOR RENT
Free Online Access.
Electric and Gas
Included. Clean!
$400/month

NEEDED! IMMEDIATE
OPENING!
COPY EQUIPMENT
REPAIRMAN

Must communicate well.
Submit application online.
Call for more details:
1-800-555-1234

Lesson 45 Name Student **Workbook**

Decode Words of Any Length

APPLICATION ACTIVITIES

A. Count the syllables in each word. Write each word in the correct column.

~~equipment~~   consonant   transit
explode   communicate   cryptogram
impossible   submit   potato
independence   vitamin   romantic

2 syllables	3 syllables	4 or more syllables
	equipment	

B. Read the words and the definitions. Circle "yes" if the definition is correct. Circle "no" if the definition is not correct.

1. Yes (No) **romantic**: a man who lives in Rome

2. Yes No   **committee**: a group of people officially delegated to perform a function

3. Yes No   **submit**: to present for the approval or consideration of another

4. Yes No   **vitamin**: a type of bug

5. Yes No   **equipment**: to give power to

6. Yes No   **explode**: to burst

Student **Workbook**   Name   Lesson 46

Compound Words

Skills Review
- Compound words are made up of two or more smaller words that are combined to make a new word (*cupcake*; *baseball*).
- A compound word may or may not be hyphenated (*show-off*; *baseball*).

DECODING

To prove compound words, separate the compound word into the individual words, and decode each word separately.

gateway   steamboat
gāte wāy   steam bōat

A. Separate the compound word into individual words. Write each word on the blank.
Example: **hillside** __hill__ __side__

1. pancake _____ _____
2. sunlight _____ _____
3. softball _____ _____
4. toenail _____ _____
5. highway _____ _____
6. peanut _____ _____

B. Now prove the words you separated in the activity above.
Example: **hillside** __hill__ __side__

READING

Read the shopping list. Notice the compound words.

Shopping List for the Holiday Weekend

handbag
lipstick
hotdogs
gumdrops
raincoat
backpack
cupcakes
peanuts

Lesson 49

Compound Words

APPLICATION ACTIVITIES

A. Fill in the blank with the correct word from the shopping list on the previous page.

1. I will frost the _____ with pink frosting.

2. When it rains, I like to wear a _____.

3. I will get mustard and ketchup to put on the _____.

4. Uncle Jed does not like _____, so he will get pretzels on the plane.

5. I think the most important make-up a woman can have is _____.

6. When we go on our hike, I will put all of the snacks in my _____ so they will be easier to carry.

B. Match the single words to create a compound word. Draw a line connecting the two.

1. week   scape
2. air   end
3. base   made
4. home   time
5. bed   ball
6. land   plane

C. In the list below, some words are compound words, and some are not. Circle all of the compound words.

sprinkle   taillight   explode   railroad

sailboat   sentence   download   jumbo

trample   handball   rabbit   cobblestone

Student Workbook Name

Most Common Words List 9

Skills Review
- Most Common Words are words that are used often when reading and sometimes do not follow phonetic skills.

Most Common Words List 9

| because | eight | these | today | give | more | such |
| through | pretty | four | away | brown | yellow | round |

A. Read the story. Circle the Most Common Words from List 9.

In some places, nature looks the same all year round. But in other places, there are four seasons to enjoy.

Where I'm from, during the first eight months of the year, the trees are either bare or green. But in the fall, the leaves are yellow and brown. The pretty colors last only about four weeks before it snows.

Today I want to go on a drive through the forest because I want to see the pretty colors of the leaves before they go away. It is such a pretty day for taking photos. I wish I could enjoy a drive on more days like these and take photos to give to my family so they can enjoy the pretty colors, too.

B. Write the missing letters to complete the Most Common Words.

1. t __ __ a y
2. e i __ h __
3. t h r o u __ __
4. b __ c a __ s e
5. g __ v __
6. y __ l l __ w
7. f o __ __
8. t h e __ __
9. p __ e t t __
10. s __ __ h
11. r o __ __ d
12. b __ o __ n
13. m o __ __
14. __ w a __

Most Common Words List 9

C. Circle the Most Common Word to complete each sentence. Write the word on the line to complete the sentence.

1. I want to go on a drive _____ I want to see the pretty colors.
   a. because   b. four
2. The trees are green for _____ months of the year.
   a. such   b. eight
3. I love days like _____.
   a. these   b. through
4. _____ I want to go on a drive.
   a. Today   b. More
5. I want to _____ some photos to my family.
   a. round   b. give
6. I wish there were _____ days like these.
   a. more   b. away
7. Today is _____ a pretty day!
   a. brown   b. such
8. I drive _____ the forest to see the trees.
   a. through   b. pretty
9. There are _____ seasons to enjoy.
   a. today   b. four
10. The colors will go _____ when it snows.
    a. away   b. these
11. The leaves are _____ and yellow in the fall.
    a. eight   b. brown
12. The trees stay green all year _____.
    a. round   b. yellow
13. It is such a _____ day!
    a. give   b. pretty
14. The leaves are brown and _____ in the fall.
    a. yellow   b. because

Student **Workbook** Name

Chapter 4
Reading in Context

Practice reading this flier using all the skills you've learned in Chapter 4. Review the words that are difficult for you. Then read the flier to a teacher or friend.

Lakeland Electric
invites you to spend Independence Day with us.

July 4, 12 p.m.–4 p.m.
Canyon Glen (right off Highway 22)

Free jumbo hotdogs and cotton candy

Softball (bats and balls provided)

Craft table with beads

Games for the little ones

Paddleboat rides on the pond

We can't wait to see you!
(map on back)

Reading in Context

Practice reading this syllabus using all the skills you've learned in Chapter 4. Review the words that are difficult for you. Then read the syllbus to a teacher or friend.

SYLLABUS

Class
Finance 201: Budgets
Tuesdays, 6 p.m.–8:30 p.m.
Fall 2012
233 Clyde Hall

Professor
Dr. Cyprus
347 Midway Hall
219-555-9271

For the next fifteen weeks, we will look at budgets in detail. You must complete this class before you proceed to other classes in the program. It will be the basis for many of them.

Attendance
Because this is a night class, we won't have as many students. As a result, we'll notice if you aren't there. Also, you'll be on a team. Your teammates will rely on you in class and outside of class. If you're absent often, it will affect your team's grade.

Come to class. If you must come late, be polite and don't disrupt the class. Respect your classmates. Don't interrupt, but don't be afraid to comment.

Grades
Your grade will be calculated in this way:
Test 1.......15%
Test 2.......15%
Test 3.......15%
Test 4.......15%
Homework*.......20%
Teamwork......20%

*Some homework will be submitted through email. This homework is due at midnight of the day indicated. All other homework must be typed and stapled. I take off 10% every day that your work is late. If you are unable to complete your homework because of a crisis, then come and talk with me.

Student Workbook   Name

Lesson 47

Murmur Diphthong AR

Skills Review

- Murmur Diphthongs make a new vowel sound when the vowels are joined with the letter *r*. It is not short or long; it has its own sound.
- The *ar* Murmur Diphthong says /ar/, which sounds like the name of the letter *r*.
- To add the suffixes *-ing*, *-ed*, *-er*, and *-est* to *ar* Murmur Diphthong words, use the rules already taught.
    1) If the word ends in a Murmur Diphthong, there is only one consonant at the end of the word, so another *r* must be added before adding the suffix (*star/starring*; *scar/scarred*).
    2) If there is a consonant following the Murmur Diphthong, there are two consonants at the end, so just add the suffix (*farm/farming*; *park/parked*).

DECODING

To mark the *ar* Murmur Diphthong:

Mark an x under the vowel *a* and arc the *ar* together. If there is a consonant after the Murmur Diphthong, do not mark it as a guardian consonant.

arm   jar

When proving *ar* Murmur Diphthong words with suffixes, prove the base word first. Then rewrite the word with the suffix and underline the suffix.

star   starring   park   parked

A. Prove these *ar* Murmur Diphthong words. Remember to mark Blends.

farm   cart   scar   yard

start   dark   card   smart

B. Prove these multi-syllabic words that contain *ar* Murmur Diphthongs.

radar   artist   margin   garden

C. Rewrite the words with the suffix.

1. bark (ed) __barked__
2. start (ing) _____
3. hard (er) _____
4. dark (est) _____

5. star (ed) _____
6. scar (ing) _____
7. farm (er) _____
8. smart (est) _____

Lesson 47 — Name

Student **Workbook**

 **Murmur Diphthong AR**

READING

Read the story. Notice the *ar* Murmur Diphthong words.

The dog barked as Carl drove into the farm yard. He could see Marge, dressed in a light coat and scarf, digging in the garden. He parked his car and walked to the large barn. Carl wanted to do his part. It would be hard, but he knew it was the smart thing to do!

APPLICATION ACTIVITIES

A. Circle the *ar* Murmur Diphthong word that best completes the sentence. Then write the word on the line. Use the story for clues.

1. Carl went to the ___*farm*___ to help Marge.

    park   (farm)   card

2. The dog began to _____ when Carl drove in.

    star   bark   hard

3. Marge wore a coat and a _____ around her neck.

    scarf   tar   yarn

4. Carl parked his _____.

    yard   scar   car

5. Carl and Marge worked in the _____.

    market   harvest   garden

B. Unscramble the words to make an *ar* Murmur Diphthong word.

1. rca _____
2. krpa _____
3. phar _____
4. rab _____
5. tsrat _____
6. nyar _____

Student Workbook Name

Lesson 47

Murmur Diphthong AR

C. Choose the correct word to complete the sentence. Use each word to complete the crossword puzzle.

Across
3. On Friday night, she is going to Tim's birthday _____. (party/alarm)
5. The boy is not stupid. He is very _____. (radar/smart)
6. After the sun goes down, it gets very _____. (harm/dark)
8. The cat and dog are inside the _____. (barn/yarn)

Down
1. Please take out the _____. It stinks! (harmony/garbage)
2. I don't live in a house. I live in an _____. (article/apartment)
4. The kids play in the _____. (yard/star)
7. If something is not easy, it is _____. (mark/hard)

Student **Workbook**   Name

Lesson 48

Murmur Diphthong OR

Skills Review
- The *or* Murmur Diphthong says /or/. It has the same sound as the word *or*.
- To add the suffixes -*ing*, -*ed*, -*er*, and -*est* to *or* Murmur Diphthong words, just add the suffix (*sort/sorting*; *form/formed*).

DECODING

To mark the *or* Murmur Diphthong:

Mark an *x* under the vowel *o* and arc the *or* together. If there is a consonant after the Murmur Diphthong, do not mark it as a guardian consonant.

for   corn

When proving *or* Murmur Diphthong words with suffixes, prove the base word first. Then rewrite the word with the suffix and underline the suffix.

sort   sorting   form   formed

A. Prove these *or* Murmur Diphthong words. Remember to mark Blends.

storm   cord   born   fork

B. Prove these multi-syllabic words that contain *or* Murmur Diphthongs.

orbit   forest   forgot   story

C. Rewrite the words with the suffix.

1. scorn (ed) ___scorned___   4. sort (ed) _____

2. form (ing) _____   5. sport (ing) _____

3. snort (ed) _____   6. cork (ed) _____

READING

Read the form. Notice the *or* Murmur Diphthong words.

IMPORT/EXPORT FORM
Important: Record all products exported from York Port.

May 8:	3,000 lbs. Cork
May 10:	5,000 lbs. Corn
May 12:	2,000 lbs. Pork
May 15:	2,500 lbs. 2" Cord
May 18:	8,000 lbs. Forest Pine

Lesson 48 Name

 Murmur Diphthong OR

APPLICATION ACTIVITIES

A. Circle two words that rhyme with the first word.

1. **corn:**	card	(torn)	(horn)
2. **pork:**	fork	park	cork
3. **cord:**	lord	Ford	lard
4. **cork:**	bark	York	stork
5. **port:**	fort	start	sort
6. **form:**	farm	dorm	storm

B. Read the words and the definitions. Circle "yes" if the definition is correct. Circle "no" if the definition is not correct.

1. Yes (No)   **forbid:** to scare
2. Yes   No   **enforce:** to make someone follow a rule or law
3. Yes   No   **ornate:** having a lot of decoration
4. Yes   No   **portray:** a tray used to hold bottles of port wine
5. Yes   No   **transport:** to move something or someone from one place to another

C. Find and circle these multi-syllabic Murmur Diphthong words in the word search. Words can go down ↓, across →, or diagonal ↘↗.

export   orbit
factory   organize
forest   popcorn
glory   report
important tornado

```
f a c t o r y s t e
p e x p o r t n z o
p a l o e r a i a f
b x a p y t n e s r
p q f c r a d a a e
o x r o g o y h d p
r c p r r r l d t o
b m o n o e q c u r
i x e l f e s f d t
t n g f w f r t o a
```

124 ReadingHorizons®

Student Workbook Name

Lesson 49

Murmur Diphthongs ER, UR, and IR

Skills Review

- The Murmur Diphthongs *er*, *ur*, and *ir* all have the same sound. They say /er/ as in *her*, *turn*, and *sir*.
- There is no easy way to decide which /er/ spelling to use. Practice remembering the correct /er/ spelling when writing the word.
- To add the suffixes *-ing*, *-ed*, *-er*, and *-est* to *er*, *ur*, and *ir* Murmur Diphthong words, use the rules already taught.
    1) If the word ends in a Murmur Diphthong, there is only one consonant at the end of the word, so another *r* must be added before adding the suffix (*stir/stirring*; *slur/slurred*).
    2) If there is a consonant following the Murmur Diphthong, there are two consonants at the end, so just add the suffix (*turn/turning*; *herd/herder*).

DECODING

To mark the *er*, *ur*, and *ir* Murmur Diphthongs:

Mark an *x* under the vowel and arc the *er*, *ur*, and *ir* together. If there is a consonant after the Murmur Diphthong, do not mark it as a guardian consonant.

her   turn   sir

When proving Murmur Diphthong words with suffixes, remember to prove the base word first. Then rewrite the word with the suffix and underline the suffix.

slur   slurred   turn   turning

A. Prove these *er*, *ur*, and *ir* Murmur Diphthong words. Remember to mark Blends.

germ   hurt   firm   verb   curb

clerk   skirt   first   stir   surf

B. Prove these multi-syllabic words that contain *er*, *ur*, and *ir* Murmur Diphthongs.

fever   hurry   circus   return   direct   winter

C. Rewrite the words with the suffix.

1. turn (ed) ___turned___
2. herd (er) _____
3. slur (ing) _____
4. surf (ed) _____
5. stir (ing) _____
6. firm (est) _____

Lesson 49

Murmur Diphthongs ER, UR, and IR

READING

Read the story. Notice the or, ur, and ir Murmur Diphthong words.

Last week, my sister made candy for the first time. As she began to stir the pan of hot syrup, it spilled onto her hand. The burn hurt a lot! I had to be her nurse and give her first aid. I didn't want any dirt to get in the burn. She was a brave girl.

APPLICATION ACTIVITIES

A. Answer the questions about the story. Circle the best answer. Write the correct answer on the line.

1. In the story, the author's _____ made candy for the first time.
   a. brother   b. sister   c. father   d. mother

2. What spilled onto her hand? _____
   a. dirt   b. a pan   c. first aid   d. hot syrup

3. How much did the burn hurt? _____
   a. very little   b. a lot   c. it didn't hurt   d. a long time

4. The author had to be a _____ and give her first aid.
   a. nurse   b. friend   c. doctor   d. mother

5. The author didn't want to get any _____ in her burn.
   a. dirt   b. syrup   c. candy   d. first aid

B. Circle the two words that rhyme with the first word.

1. **skirt:**   start   (hurt)   (flirt)
2. **clerk:**   lurk   cork   jerk
3. **burn:**   turn   stun   concern
4. **germ:**   affirm   perm   reform
5. **fur:**   fear   stir   her
6. **bird:**   purred   bride   stirred

Student **Workbook**   Name

Lesson 49

Murmur Diphthongs ER, UR, and IR

C. Read each sentence about a different kind of worker. Complete the sentence with a word from the box. Each word is used only once.

| computer | dirt | hammer |
| meter | sermon | tigers |

1. A cab driver uses a _____ to determine the price of a ride.

2. A carpenter uses a _____ to drive a nail.

3. A circus performer uses _____ to entertain people.

4. A clergyman uses a _____ to uplift people.

5. A clerk uses a _____ to record sales.

6. A gardener uses _____ to plant seeds.

D. Read these signs. Circle the words that contain a Murmur Diphthong that has the sound /er/. There are four. Draw a box around one word that has an *ar* Murmur Diphthong.

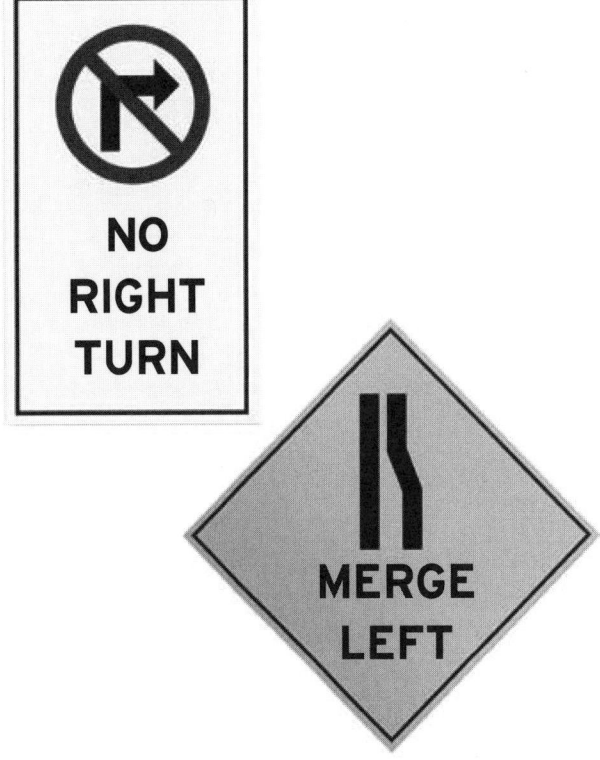

Student Workbook   Name _____   Lesson 50

Exceptions to Murmur Diphthongs

Skills Review
- There are some exceptions to Murmur Diphthongs. Each exception will be reviewed below.

DECODING

Exceptions 1 and 2
   When silent *e* comes right after a Murmur Diphthong, the silent *e* will rule (the vowel will be long). When an adjacent vowel comes right before the Murmur Diphthong, the adjacent vowel will rule (the vowel will be long). Mark the words according to Phonetic Skill 4 and Phonetic Skill 5. (Do not mark the Murmur Diphthong in the word because it does not make a Murmur Diphthong sound.)

   A silent *e* at the end of a Murmur Diphthong word will not change the sound of the Murmur Diphthong if there is a consonant between the Murmur Diphthong and silent *e* (*nurse*).

   When *c* or *g* follows a Murmur Diphthong, you will still mark it as a bridge.

A. Prove these words.

   fire   large   force   curve   clear

Exception 3
   When *ea* comes before *r* and another consonant, the *r* changes the sound to /er/. Mark the *a* silent and put an arc under the *ear*.

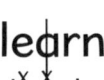

B. Prove these words.

   heard   early

Exception 4 ("Crazy *W*")
   When *a* follows *w*, the vowel changes to the short *o* sound. Mark a small *o* with the short vowel mark above the *a* to show the sound. When *ar* follows *w*, it will have the sound of /or/. Put a small *or* above the *ar*. When *or* follows *w*, it will have the sound of /er/. Put a small *er* above the *or*. Because *qu* has the *w* sound, the same vowel sound changes will apply.

Lesson 50 **Exceptions to Murmur Diphthongs**

C. Prove these words.

wand   warp   world

Exception 5
Sometimes, *ar* and *er* sound like the word "air." Some words end in *-ary* and *-ery*. The ending *-ary* has the sound /air-y/. Words that end in *-ery* have the sound /air-y/ or /er-y/.

To prove words that have *-ary* and *-ery* endings, mark the Murmur Diphthong and the *y*. If it has the sound /air-y/, put a little "air" above the Murmur Diphthong, and put a long *e* above the *y*.

D. Prove these words.

berry   parent

Exception 6
Sometimes, *or* and *ar* in unstressed syllables have the sound /er/. Put a small *er* above the Murmur Diphthong to help you remember how to pronounce it.

E. Prove these words.

favor   major

READING

Read the magazine article. Notice the words that are Exceptions to Murmur Diphthongs.

This was by far the worst forest fire Marge had ever seen! She had been a nurse in the military and was now doing some charity work at the fire camp. She did whatever she could to help, which included serving the firefighters their meals.

A large squad of firefighters wandered into the tent for something to eat. Marge knew they would need lots of water to drink in addition to the huge quantity of hot waffles and ham the cook had made, and she hurried to serve them. They ate as if they were about to starve!

Marge listened as they spoke. She heard them say that there was some fear that their workforce was too small. They decided to warn their director of the need to hire more firefighters.

Student **Workbook**   Name

Exceptions to Murmur Diphthongs

Lesson 50

APPLICATION ACTIVITIES

A. Use the magazine article on the previous page for the following activities:
  1) Circle the exceptions where silent *e* or adjacent vowels are overriding the Murmur Diphthong.
  2) Put a box around those words that follow Exception 4 — "Crazy *W*".

B. Choose the word from the box that best completes the sentence.

warn	monastery	score
ferry	early	inherit
library	carve	bribery

1. Jon decided to go to bed _____ since he didn't feel well.

2. Jenny took a _____ across the harbor.

3. The monks preferred the seclusion and peace of living in a _____.

4. The rich woman's children will _____ a lot of money when she dies.

5. The policeman tried to _____ the students about the dangers of drinking and driving.

6. At the skating competition, the judges were looking for the highest _____ to award the first place trophy.

7. The couple decided to _____ their initials into the tree.

C. Circle the word that follows the exception.

1. Exception 1 (silent *e*)   farm   fire
2. Exception 2 (adjacent vowel)   fair   fern
3. Exception 3 (*ear* sounds like /er/) fear   learn
4. Exception 4 ("Crazy *W*")   warm   went
5. Exception 5 (*er* or *ar* sounds like /air/) merry   mart
6. Exception 6 (*or* or *ar* sounds like /er/ in an unstressed syllable)   flavor   horn

ReadingHorizons®

131

Lesson 50   Name   **Student Workbook**

Exceptions to Murmur Diphthongs

D. Add the suffixes to the words. Remember to drop the *e* before adding the suffix. Then complete the crossword puzzle.

Across
3. splurge + ed = _____
4. fire + ed = _____
5. nurse + ing = _____

Down
1. wire + ed = _____
2. merge + ing = _____
3. stare + ing = _____

E. Draw a line from a word on the left to a word on the right to create a compound word that contains a Murmur Diphthong.

1. post   corn

2. home   port

3. air   card

4. pop   line

5. under   work

Student **Workbook**   Name

Most Common Words List 10

Skills Review
- Most Common Words are words that are used often when reading and sometimes do not follow phonetic skills.

Most Common Words List 10

| goes | great | says | move | does | mother | build |
| father | should | answer | learn | eye | thought | together |

A. Read the story. Circle the Most Common Words from List 10.

My father wants to build a new house on his own. The problem is he does not know how. He says the best way to learn is by doing. So, each Saturday he goes to a community class to learn how to build a house. He likes that the teacher can answer any of his questions.

He was having such a great time learning one day that he thought he should get my mother involved. He thinks it would be a fun project to work on together. My mother, on the other hand, only wants to help once they move into the house. She has no interest in helping to build the house. But she has a good eye for decorating!

B. Answer the questions about the story above.

1. Who wants to build a house? _____
2. What is the problem? _____
3. How is he learning how to build a house? _____
4. What does he like about the class? _____
5. Who does not want to help until they move in? _____

Most Common Words List 10

C. Find the Most Common Words from List 10 in the word search. Words can go down ↓, across →, or diagonal ↘ ↗.

```
r m o v e f t a s
a q o l e a r n w
l b h t e t t e i
s l u r h h y a g
a i g i g e e e o
y s o u l r r t e
s h o u l d o e s
e h a n s w e r o
t o g e t h e r v
```

goes	move	build	answer	thought
great	does	father	learn	together
says	mother	should	eye	

D. Unscramble the letters to form a Most Common Word.
    Example: **sgeo**   _goes_

1. sluhod _____

2. deso _____

3. theergot _____

4. yee _____

5. snawre _____

6. soge _____

7. veom _____

8. dubil _____

9. nrael _____

10. asys _____

11. throme _____

12. treag _____

13. outghth _____

14. threaf _____

Digraphs CH, SH, WH, TH, and TH

Lesson 51

Skills Review

- Digraphs are two consonants that stand together but make only *one* consonant sound (ma*th*; *ch*at).
- Digraphs are joined with an arc and do not split in multi-syllabic words.
- Digraphs can begin or end words (*sh*ut; wi*sh*).
- The new consonant sounds are *ch* (as in *ch*urch and su*ch*), *sh* (as in *sh*irt and di*sh*), *wh* (as in *wh*eel and *wh*ite), *th* voiceless (as in *th*ink and ba*th*), and *th* voiced (as in *th*is and *th*at). (Note: To pronounce *wh* correctly, air should blow softly from the mouth when saying the sound.)
- If a silent *e* comes after the *th* Digraph, it makes the vowel long (cloth/cloth*e*; bath/bath*e*).
- When a *short* vowel sound is heard right before the /ch/ sound, the *ch* will be spelled *tch* (ma*tch*; pi*tch*). Exceptions: rich, much, which, such, touch.
- Sometimes, the *ch* sounds like /sh/ (*ch*ef) or /k/ (*ch*ord).

DECODING

Arc the consonants together that make a Digraph.

chip   ship   whip   thin   then   clothe

Note: Mark a ‿ under the *th* to show that it is voiceless. Mark a ∿ under the *th* to show that it is voiced.

thin   then

When a Digraph ends a one-syllable word, mark it with only one guardian consonant because it makes only one sound.

much   mash   math

If a word that ends in a Digraph has another guardian consonant before it, mark the word with two guardian stars.

ranch   match

A. Prove these words.

beach   cash   bathe   whine   lunch

shirt   church   thing   itch   she

B. Prove these multi-syllabic words that contain Digraphs. Remember that Digraphs do not split.

beneath   chapter   sharpen   whimper   athlete

Lesson 51 Name **Student Workbook**

 Digraphs CH, SH, WH, TH, and TH

C. Rewrite each word with the suffix.

1. mash (ed) _mashed_   4. march (ed) _____

2. wish (ing) _____ 5. ranch (er) _____

3. pinch (ed) _____ 6. coach (ing) _____

READING

Read this ad. Notice the words with Digraphs.

Shop our ads! Check our cheap prices!

 Add charm to your dish shelf without crashing your budget!

 Check the size chart. Get one while they last! These wash and wear t-shirts are a must!

 Thin chips! Ranch or cheddar!

 Wish your hair would shine? It will when you use this brush!

 This bench can also be used as a chest. Seat opens to store blankets, sheets, and toys. The seat will latch shut.

 Get in shape while taking the dog for a short walk each day using your new dog leash!

APPLICATION ACTIVITIES

A. Circle the word that has the Digraph specified.

1. **ch**: Add charm to your dish shelf without crashing your budget!

2. **wh**: Check the size chart. Get one while they last!

3. **sh**: Seat opens to store blankets, sheets, and toys.

4. **th**: Thin chips! Ranch or cheddar!

5. **th**: These wash and wear t-shirts are a must!

Student Workbook Name _____ Lesson 51

Digraphs *CH*, *SH*, *WH*, *TH*, and *TH*

B. Replace the Digraph in the word with another Digraph to make another real word. Use *ch*, *sh*, *wh*, or *th*.
   Example: why   _s_ _h_ y

1. chip   ___ ___ i p   4. shine   ___ ___ i n e
2. then   ___ ___ e n   5. shop   ___ ___ o p
3. thin   ___ ___ i n   6. with   w i ___ ___

C. These words contain voiced and voiceless *th* Digraphs. Write the words with a **voiceless** *th* under the "Voiceless (⌣)" column. Write the words with a **voiced** *th* under the "Voiced (⌢)" column.

~~athlete~~   math   mother   thank   this

these   thin   thirty   then   bother

Voiceless (⌣)	Voiced (⌢)
athlete	

Student Workbook — Lesson 52

More Digraphs PH, GN, KN, CK, and WR

Skills Review
- *Ph, gn, kn, ck,* and *wr* are new spellings for sounds already learned.
- *Ph* says /f/ (*phone*); *gn* says /n/ (*gnome*); *kn* says /n/ (*knee*); *ck* says /k/ (*back*); *wr* says /r/ (*write*).
- The Digraph *ck* always ends a word or syllable. It is used with short vowel sounds. The *c* and *k* are never separated in multi-syllabic words (*chick-en*; *pick-le*).
- When the Digraph *gn* comes at the end of a word and comes after *i*, the sound of *gn* is still /n/, and the *i* is long (*sign*).

DECODING

To mark the Digraph, arc the consonants together that make the Digraph. (Note: To help you remember the pronunciation of these Digraphs, write a small *f* over the *ph* Digraph. Draw a line down through the silent letter in the *gn*, *kn*, and *wr* Digraphs.)

The *c* and *k* are never separated in multi-syllabic words.

When the Digraph *gn* comes at the end of a word:
1) Mark the vowel *i* with an *x*.
2) Place an arc under the *gn* Digraph.
3) Mark the *g* silent.
4) Since *ign* works like a vowel family, underline *ign*.
5) Mark the *i* long.

A. Circle the Digraphs in these words.

sti(ck)   knee   phase   gnash   sock   wrong   assign

B. Prove these words that have Digraphs.

black   kneel   graph   gnarl

wreck   knock   wrist   quick

C. Prove these multi-syllabic words that contain Digraphs. Remember that Digraphs do not split.

photo   pocket   written   digraph   align

Lesson 52 Name   Student **Workbook**

More Digraphs *PH, GN, KN, CK,* and *WR*

D. Prove these compound words that contain Digraphs. Divide the words first. Then decode them.

lipstick   nickname   checkup

padlock   payphone

READING

Read this ad. Notice the words with Digraphs.

Your pipes need a wrench like this one! Phone in your order.

Keep your truck running like a clock. Use Truck Track at the first sign of anything wrong.

Check out this sharp buy!

Great pocket knife.

Every athlete needs to get the Knack to protect knees, wrists, and shins from injury.

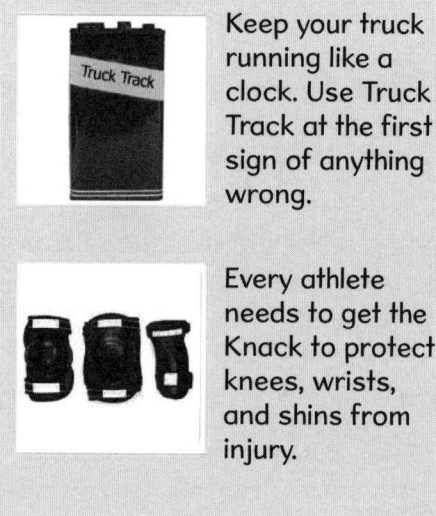

APPLICATION ACTIVITIES

A. Circle the word that has the Digraph specified.

1. **ph:** Need a place to store your photos? Use "Snap Trap"!

2. **gn:** Keep gnats away with "Fly Away" bug spray.

3. **kn:** Great pocket knife.

4. **ck:** Check our good deals!

5. **wr:** Use "Truck Track" at the first sign of anything wrong.

Lesson 52

More Digraphs PH, GN, KN, CK, and WR

B. Circle the Digraph word that best completes the sentence. Then write the word in the blank. Use the pictures as clues.

1. The chef needed a sharp __knife__ to cut the onion.

    block   (knife)   pick

2. The mechanic used a _____ to fix the car.

    wrench   knot   rock

3. Jane hung a _____ on the front door for the holidays.

    lock   knob   wreath

4. She heard a _____ at the door, so she went to see who it was.

    knock   wrist   gnome

C. Unscramble each of the words. Use the sentences as clues. Write the words in the boxes.

1. **k e n d a**

    If you make bread, you have to _____ the dough.

2. **p o n h y**

    If something is fake, it is _____.

3. **h y d b a i r t**

    If it is your _____, you are celebrating the day you were born.

4. **k o m h e s c i**

    If you miss home, you are _____.

5. **t l c i s k i p**

    A type of make-up women wear on their lips is _____.

Lesson 52

More Digraphs *PH*, *GN*, *KN*, *CK*, and *WR*

6. r o t h a o p p h g | | | | | | | | | |
                                    5

If you take a picture, you take a _____.

D. Now copy the letters in the numbered boxes to the boxes below with the same number to reveal a new word.

CLUE: What word is short for the word "photograph"?

1	2	3	4	5

Student Workbook   Name   Lesson 53

Digraph Blends

Skills Review
- When the Blend letters *l*, *r*, or *s* are added after certain Digraphs, a *Digraph Blend* is formed.
- All three letters are joined with an arc.
- *R* added to the Digraphs *sh* and *th* form the Blends *shr* and *thr* (*shr*imp; *thr*ee).
- *L* and *r* can be added to the Digraph *ph* (*ph*lox; *ph*rase).
- All three Blend letters can be added to the Digraph *ch*. When added, they change the sound of the Digraph from a /ch/ sound to a /k/ sound (*ch*loride; *ch*rome; s*ch*eme).

DECODING

Put an arc under the consonants that make a Digraph Blend. All three letters are joined with an arc.

            phrase

A. Prove these words.

chrome   phlox   shrink   throne

B. Prove these multi-syllabic words. Remember that Digraphs do not split.

arthritis   chloride   shrubbery   thrifty

READING

Read this story. Notice words with Digraph Blends.

Grant drove slowly through the park. Three little thrush sang their shrill song. Purple phlox and shrubbery dotted the path. The faint odor of chlorine from the nearby pool filled Grant's nose and tickled his throat. It would be so nice to stop and take a nap, but that was not in the scheme of things! Today he must polish the chrome on his car and adjust the throttle!

Lesson 53 — Name — *Student Workbook*

Digraph Blends

APPLICATION ACTIVITIES

A. In the story on the prevoius page, there is one sentence that has three words containing Digraph Blends. Write that sentence here.

_____

_____

B. Match the word to the best definition. Use the context from the story as clues.

1. throng — having a sharp, high sound
2. thrush — shiny, gray metal used on cars
3. phlox — a type of plant that has flowers on it
4. shrill — a small song bird
5. scheme — a large number of people crowded together
6. chrome — a plan of action

C. Unscramble the letters to make a real word. Hint: All the words contain a Digraph Blend and were used in Activity B.

1. xlhpo _____

2. rmoche _____

3. llrshi _____

4. echsme _____

5. rhtsuh _____

144 ReadingHorizons®

Student Workbook   Name   Lesson 54

Digraph Words with Plural Endings

Skills Review
- A plural means more than one. To form a plural, *s* or *es* is added to the end of a word. (Remember that to form a plural, add an *s* to most words ending in a consonant and an *es* to words ending in *s*, *ss*, *zz*, or *x* [hat<u>s</u>; dress<u>es</u>; buzz<u>es</u>; box<u>es</u>].)
- Add the plural *es* to words ending with the Digraphs *ch* or *sh* (church<u>es</u>; wish<u>es</u>).

DECODING

When adding the plural ending:
1) Prove the base word first.
2) Rewrite the word with the ending.
3) Underline the ending.

   dish<u>es</u>   peach   peach<u>es</u>

A. Underline the plural ending in each word.

    beaches   churches   pitches   watches

B. Prove the base word. Rewrite the word with the plural ending. Then underline the plural ending.
Example: dish   <u>dishes</u>

1. wish _____

2. coach _____

3. ranch _____

4. teach _____

5. witch _____

6. match _____

Lesson 54 — Digraph Words with Plural Endings

APPLICATION ACTIVITIES

A. Choose the word from the box that fits best to complete the poem.

benches	coaches	witches
crashes	peaches	wishes

My friend and I needed to take a day off.
We decided to hit the beaches.
We packed a lunch with all sorts of food,
Including a bag of ripe _____.
                                  1.

We couldn't find the entrance to the first beach.
We kept running into high trenches.
We decided to simply jump them,
And set up our stuff near one of the _____.
                                                  2.

We had a great day just relaxing —
No homework or washing dishes.
We swam, took a nap, and just talked.
I had been granted one of my fondest _____!
                                                   3.

B. Circle all of the words that need an *es* to make them plural.

hat   (ash)   ranch   brick   bunch

lunch   car   match   plate   wish

Most Common Words List 11

Skills Review
- Most Common Words are words that are used often when reading and sometimes do not follow phonetic skills.

Most Common Words List 11

both   carry   friend   once   sure   color
enough   always   young   though   talk

A. Read the story. Circle the Most Common Words from List 11.

My best friend lives 300 miles away, but we talk on the phone every week. We are able to carry on a conversation for hours. But we both decided not to talk to each other for more than an hour at a time, though we always have enough to talk about. We just have to be sure we don't go over our cell phone minutes. That can be expensive!

Once, we talked for three hours without stopping! We lost track of time talking about our young children, our favorite color of paint for a bedroom, and how we weren't sure what to cook for dinner. Our cell phone bills cost a lot that month!

B. Answer the questions about the story. Circle the best answer.

1. Who lives 300 miles away?

    a. her sister   c. her children

    b. her mother   d. her best friend

2. What do they do every week?

    a. walk together   c. talk on the phone

    b. e-mail each other   d. visit each other's homes

Most Common Words List 11

3. True or false: They don't talk for more than an hour because they run out of things to talk about.

   a. true   b. false

4. In the story, the author said they talk about all of the following EXCEPT:

   a. their children   c. where they go shopping

   b. what to cook for dinner   d. what color of paint they like for a bedroom

5. Why did their cell phone bills cost a lot?

   a. They talked every day.   c. They forgot to hang up the phone.

   b. They talked for three hours.   d. They were calling long distance from different countries.

6. You can guess that the author of this passage is

   a. male.   c. a child.

   b. female.   d. very old.

C. One of the words in each set is a Most Common Word, and the other is a nonsense word. Circle the Most Common Word.

   Example: both   bith

1. lkat	talk	7. caryr	carry
2. ghenou	enough	8. young	gnouy
3. drenif	friend	9. slawy	always
4. both	thob	10. sure	resu
5. color	roclo	11. thugho	though
6. once	coen		

Student Workbook

Lesson 55

Special Vowel Sounds AU/AW, OU/OW, OI/OY

Skills Review

- Special Vowel Sounds have their own sounds, and they are *not* adjacent vowels.
- Special Vowel Sounds are marked with an *x* between the two vowels and are then joined with an arc.
- Special Vowel Sounds *au* and *aw*: Both spellings have the same sound, /aw/, as in the words *fault* and *saw*. *Au* is not used at the end of a word. Use *aw* at the end of a word.
- Special Vowel Sounds *ou* and *ow*: Both spellings have the same sound, /ow/, as in the words *count* and *cow*. *Ow* has another sound, long *o*, such as in the word *snow*. The spelling *ou* is not used at the end of the word except the words *you* and *thou*. (The spelling *ou* has other sounds: /oo/ as in *could*; short *u* as in *touch*; long *o* as in *soul*; /oo/ as in *youth*; and /aw/ as in *cough*, *thought*.) Spell with *ow* at the end of a word.
- Special Vowel Sounds *oi* and *oy*: Both spellings have the same sound, /oy/, as in the words *coin* and *boy*. *Oi* is not used at the end of a word. Use *oy* at the end of a word.

DECODING

Special Vowel Sounds are marked with an *x* between the two vowels and are then joined with an arc.

haunt   cloud   oil

saw   how   boy

If *ow* says ō, place a long vowel mark above the *o*.

slōw   bōwl

A. Mark the Special Vowel Sound in each word.

hawk   low   point   cow   boy

B. Prove these words. Remember to mark the Blends and Digraphs.

straw   blow   shout   moist   launch

now   joy   vault   show   oil

Lesson 55

Special Vowel Sounds AU/AW, OU/OW, OI/OY

Student **Workbook**

READING

Read this e-mail. Notice the words with Special Vowel Sounds.

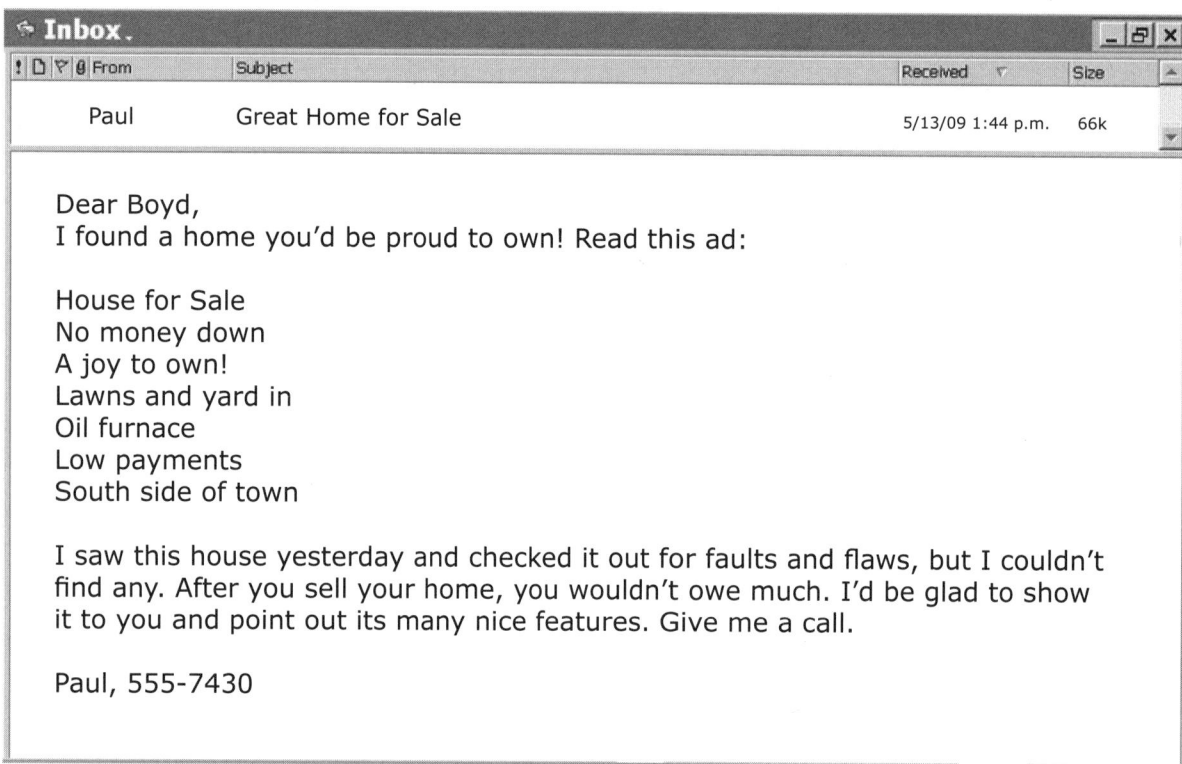

APPLICATION ACTIVITIES

A. Answer the questions about the e-mail above. Circle the best answer.

1. What is for sale?

    a. a car   c. a house

    b. a bed   d. a camera

2. The e-mail mentioned all of these positive things about this home EXCEPT:

    a. free utilities.   c. the lawn and yard have been put in.

    b. low payments.   d. you don't need to put any money down.

3. True or false: This home has many faults and flaws.

    a. true   b. false

Special Vowel Sounds AU/AW, OU/OW, OI/OY

4. Boyd is probably

    a. someone who sells homes.

    b. someone who fixes homes.

    c. someone who wants to buy a home.

    d. someone who is trying to sell his home.

5. Paul is probably

    a. someone who sells homes.

    b. someone who fixes homes.

    c. someone who wants to buy a home.

    d. someone who is trying to sell his home.

B. Write the correct word from the box to complete each sentence.

pound	grow	boil	hoist
thaw	soil	plow	haul

1. You need to _____ the water before adding the pasta.

2. You need to _____ the frozen meat before cooking it.

3. The meat is on sale for $1.99 a _____ this week.

4. The farmer needs to _____ the field before planting.

5. He had to prepare the _____ before planting seeds in it.

6. This is the time of year the crops begin to _____.

7. They used a rope to _____ the piano up to the second floor of the apartment building.

8. I have to _____ the garbage in my trailer to the dump.

Special Vowel Sounds AU/AW, OU/OW, OI/OY

C. Find and circle these words that contain Special Vowel Sounds in the word search. Words can go down ↓, across →, or diagonal ↘ ↗.

coil   crawl   out   show
toy   coin   haunt   proud
town   yawn

b	p	d	g	y	e	a	d
c	b	p	h	a	w	y	k
h	c	r	a	w	l	q	r
g	o	o	u	n	s	c	q
i	i	u	n	g	h	o	n
n	l	d	t	t	o	i	a
s	l	r	t	o	w	n	n
r	z	j	e	y	f	p	o

Student **Workbook** Name Lesson 56

Special Vowel Sounds *OO* and *OO*

Skills Review
- Special Vowel Sounds (SVS) have their own sounds, and they are *not* adjacent vowels.
- Special Vowel Sounds are marked with an *x* between the two vowels and are then joined with an arc.
- Special Vowel Sound *oo*: The double *o* has two sounds. It has the sound /oo/, as in *look*, and the sound /oo/, as in *zoo*.

DECODING

Special Vowel Sounds are marked with an *x* between the two vowels and are then joined with an arc.

hook   zoo

A. Mark the Special Vowel Sound in these words.

book   cool   cook   room   moon

B. Prove these words that have Special Vowel Sounds. Remember to mark Blends and Digraphs.

spool   shook   boost   tooth

spoon   foot   wood   stood

READING

Thoughts of a chef just before a cooking contest:

Read this paragraph. Notice the words with *oo* Special Vowel Sounds.

"Oh, no! I think I left my favorite spoon on the stool at the cooking school. Now what should I do? A good cook, like a good wood worker, must use the right tools! Oh, well. My cooking does leave room for improvement. I'll just get a new cookbook as soon as I can and perhaps find a dish that will please the judge's sweet tooth!"

Lesson 56 Name Student **Workbook**

Special Vowel Sounds OO and OO

APPLICATION ACTIVITIES

A. Answer the questions about the reading on the previous page.

1. What did the chef forget? _____

2. Where did he leave it? _____

3. He said that good cooks must have the right _____.

4. He said he would get a new _____.

5. He hoped to please the judge's sweet _____.

B. Cross out the word that does not have the same *oo* sound as the first word in the set.

1. **spoon:**	moon	pool	tooth	~~good~~
2. **book:**	brook	stool	wood	foot
3. **cool:**	fool	smooth	hook	proof
4. **boot:**	foot	tool	soon	mood
5. **wood:**	stood	broom	hood	cook
6. **foot:**	shook	took	food	look

C. Match the word with the correct definition.

1. boost — a black, European crow

2. crook — to bend head and shoulders forward and down

3. rook — to lift or raise by pushing from behind or below

4. stoop — a dishonest person; thief

Student **Workbook** Name

Lesson 56

Special Vowel Sounds *OO* and *OO*

D. Write the words that have the sound /oo/ as in *zoo* in column 1. Write the words that have the sound /oo/ as in *look* in column 2.

~~pool~~	~~hood~~	foot	book	room	tooth
booth	tool	smooth	snooze	spoon	cool
wood	shook	cook	hook	broom	mood
school	troop	too	brook	stool	stood

1 "zoo"	2 "look"
pool	hood

Student Workbook Name _____

Lesson 57

More Special Vowel Sound Skills

Skills Review
- When adding a suffix to a word with a Special Vowel Sound, just add the suffix (*boil/boiling*; *haunt/haunted*).
- Special Vowel Sounds are found in multi-syllabic words.
- Some Special Vowel Sound words are contained in compound words (*football*; *fishbowl*; *cookout*).

DECODING

Divide the multi-syllabic words according to the skills that have been taught.

Divide compound words between the two words, and decode each word separately.

A. Prove these words.

destroy   laundry   profound   powder

bamboo   authentic   typhoon   thyroid

scoundrel   employment

B. Prove these compound words.

footprint   outside   moonbeam   bookmark

teaspoon   jawbone   snowball   townhouse

READING

Read these newspaper headlines. Notice the words with Special Vowel Sound skills.

Lesson 57 — More Special Vowel Sound Skills

APPLICATION ACTIVITIES

A. Fill in the blank with the missing Special Vowel Sound word from newspaper headlines on the previous page.

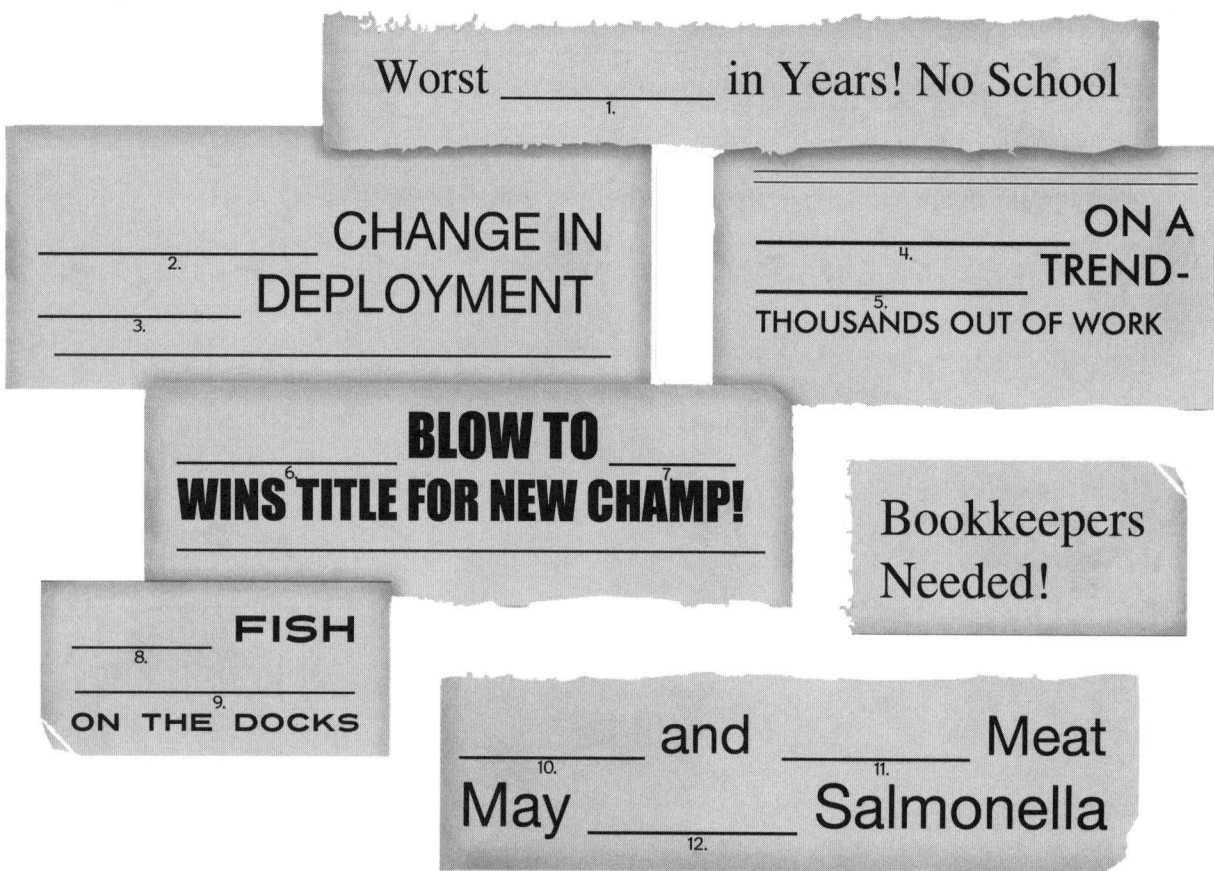

Worst _____ in Years! No School
1.

_____ CHANGE IN DEPLOYMENT
2.
_____
3.

_____ ON A _____ TREND-
4.
_____
5.
THOUSANDS OUT OF WORK

_____ BLOW TO _____ WINS TITLE FOR NEW CHAMP!
6. 7.

Bookkeepers Needed!

_____ FISH
8.
_____
ON THE 9. DOCKS

_____ and _____ Meat
10. 11.
May _____ Salmonella
12.

B. Circle the words that are compound words. Then draw a line to show where the words separate.

broom	stick	goodnight	cauliflower	doghouse
haunting	checkbook	housewife	soybean
destroy	pauper	downtown	exploit
toothbrush	playground	rowboat	

C. Write a sentence using at least <u>two</u> words from the words in Activity B.

_____

_____

_____

Most Common Words List 12

Skills Review
- Most Common Words are words that are used often when reading and sometimes do not follow phonetic skills.

Most Common Words List 12

| door | heard | early | toward | love | money |
| done | beauty | nothing | busy | laugh | |

A. Read the story. Then circle the Most Common Words from List 12.

I love to throw a party for my friends during the holidays, even though it is a very busy time of year and it can cost a lot of money for all of the food and decorations.

One time, when I was almost finished making the preparations for a party, I heard a knock on the door. Had someone arrived early? As I walked toward the door, I realized I had done nothing to get myself ready! I was so busy getting the food ready for the party that I forgot about getting myself ready! Oh, well! So much for my own beauty at my own party! I just had to laugh it off.

B. Circle the correct Most Common Word to complete the sentence. Then write the word in the blank.

1. I haven't ___done___ anything to get ready for the party.
   beauty   early   (done)

2. I have _____ to wear to the party.
   early   done   nothing

3. I _____ a knock at the door.
   laugh   heard   beauty

4. I _____ to throw a party.
   laugh   heard   love

Most Common Words List 12

5. I walked _____ the door.

   toward   done   nothing

6. I am very _____ preparing for the party.

   busy   love   toward

7. Someone had arrived _____ to the party.

   money   busy   early

8. Sometimes I just _____ at myself to keep from crying.

   done   laugh   beauty

9. It costs a lot of _____.

   busy   money   early

10. We all have _____ within us.

    heard   beauty   toward

11. There was a knock at the _____.

    door   busy   money

Most Common Words List 12

C. Complete the crossword puzzle using the Most Common Words from List 12. Use the sentences from the story as clues.

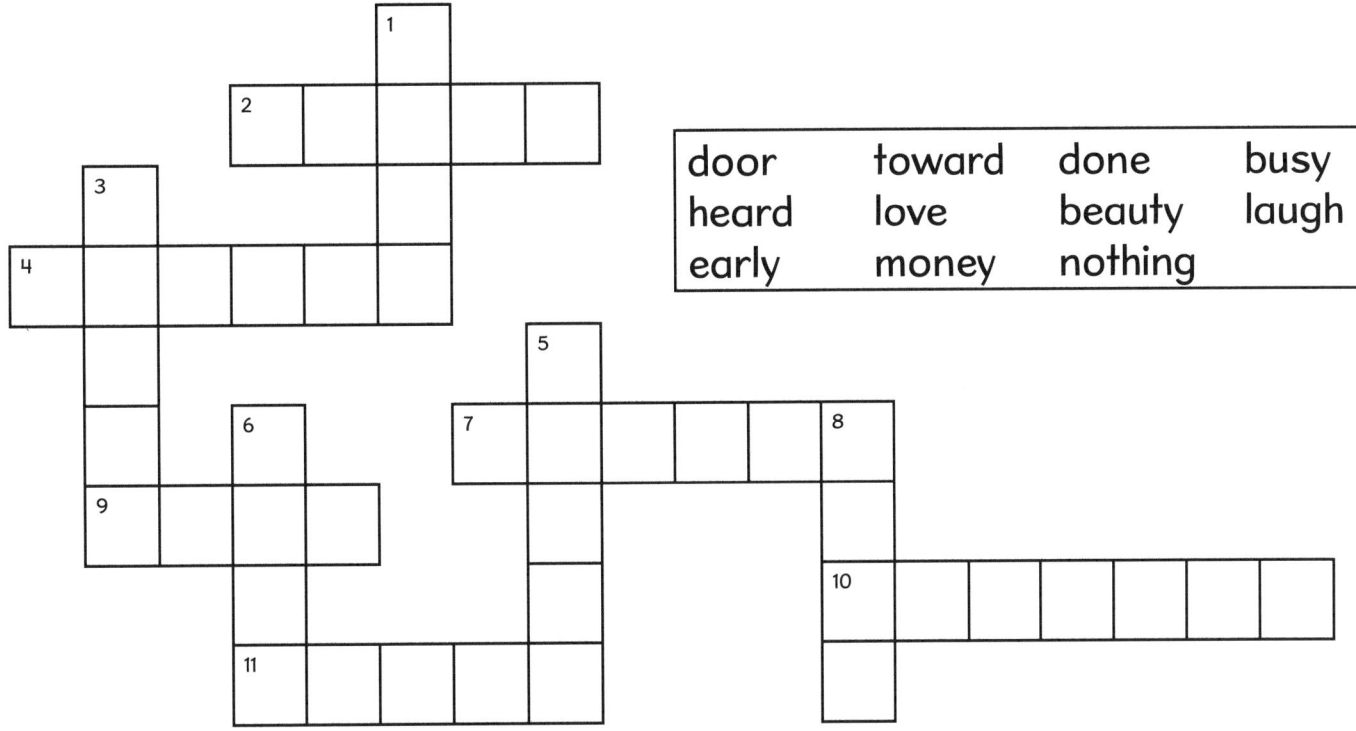

door   toward   done   busy
heard love   beauty laugh
early money   nothing

Across

2. I just had to _____ it off.
4. So much for my own _____ at my own party!
7. I walked _____ the door.
9. I walked toward the _____.
10. I have _____ to wear to the party.
11. Had someone arrived _____?

Down

1. I was so _____ getting the food ready for the party.
3. I _____ a knock at the door.
5. It costs a lot of _____.
6. I _____ to throw a party for my friends during the holidays.
8. I had _____ nothing to get myself ready!

Student **Workbook**   Name

Lesson 58

Other Suffixes

Skills Review

- A suffix is one or more letters added to the end of a word that change the meaning of the word and usually its part of speech.
- **-TION**: This combination has the sound /shun/. It always comes at the end of a word and is its own syllable (sta*tion*; atten*tion*).
- **-SION**: This combination has the sound /shun/ and /zhun/. It says /shun/ when an *s*, *n*, or *l* come right before the -*sion* (permi*ssion*). It says /zhun/ when a vowel or Murmur Diphthong comes right before the -*sion* (le*sion*; excur*sion*).
- Whenever the vowel *i* comes right before -*tion* and -*sion*, the sound of *i* will be short.
- **-TIAL**: This suffix has the sound /shul/ (par*tial*).
- **-US** and **-OUS**: Both endings have the sound /us/. Words ending in -*us* are nouns and words ending in -*ous* are adjectives (camp*us*, fam*ous*).
- **-IST** and **-EST**: Words ending in -*ist* are usually nouns and words ending in -*est* are usually adjectives (dent*ist*; slow*est*).

DECODING

To mark words with -*tion*, -*sion*, and -*tial* suffixes, place an *x* under the two vowels, and join the three or four letters together with an arc.

To prove words that have -*ous* suffixes, place an *x* under and between the two vowels, and draw an arc under all three letters.

To prove words that have -*us*, -*ist*, or -*est* suffixes, just underline the suffix.

    circ<u>us</u>   dent<u>ist</u>   long<u>est</u>

A. Prove these words.

adoption	caption	detention	explosion
fiction	isolation	vacation	reflection
famous	artist	cactus	shortest

Lesson 58 — Name

Other Suffixes

READING

Read this letter. Notice the words with Other Suffixes.

> Dear Fred,
>   It is hard to describe the destruction that resulted from the explosion at the mine. The injured men were moved to a safe location. Emotions ran high. I was so nervous. The doctor said an amputation might be necessary. We were all joyous when that was not the case. The doctor did a fabulous job. Ted's leg is all stitched up, cast, and in traction. We have permission to visit him anytime. The other men suffered only minor abrasions. The community has given tremendous help. Perhaps our little mine will now be famous! I'll write more later.
>
>   Sincerely,
>   Dan

APPLICATION ACTIVITIES

A. Answer the questions about the reading above.

1. What caused all the destruction at the mine? _____

2. What did Dan say "ran high"? _____

3. What did the doctor say might be necessary for Ted's leg?

   _____

4. The other men suffered only what? _____

5. What did Dan think their little mine might be now? _____

Student **Workbook**   Name

Lesson 58

Other Suffixes

B. Write the words below in the correct column. If the word ending with *-tion* or *-sion* sounds like /shun/, write it in the "/shun/" column. If the *-sion* sounds like /zhun/, write it in the "/zhun/" column. (Letters between "/ /" represent sounds.)

~~illusion~~   fiction   submersion   emotion

mission   vision   condition   confusion

/shun/	/zhun/
	illusion

C. (Circle) the words that are nouns. Underline the words that are adjectives. (Remember that words ending in *-us* are nouns and words ending in *-ous* are adjectives.)

(bonus)   <u>enormous</u>   joyous   surplus

artist   shortest   weakest   orthodontist

fungus   tallest   obvious   cyclist

circus   dentist   fattest   famous

D. Choose and write in the correct ending for each word. Use the context as clues. (Remember that a noun names a person, place, thing, or idea and an adjective describes a noun.)

1. He is the tall__*est*__ man I've ever seen. (est/ist)

2. He is a very fam_____ athlete. (ous/us)

3. Have you been to the dent_____ to get your teeth cleaned? (est/ist)

Other Suffixes

4. It makes me nerv_____ to have someone work on my teeth! (ous/us)

5. My brother wants to become a biolog_____, so he is studying biology in college right now. (est/ist)

6. He said the college camp_____ is very big. (ous/us)

7. After she paid her bills, she had a surpl_____ of $500 at the end of the month. (ous/us)

8. She is the smart_____ person I know when it comes to finances. (est/ist)

Student Workbook Name   Lesson 59

Adding Suffixes to Words Ending in Y

Skills Review

- When a word ends in an *adjacent vowel* with *y*, just add an *s* to form plurals or verb endings (*day<u>s</u>*; *key<u>s</u>*).
- When *y* follows a *consonant* at the end of the word, the *y* must be changed to *i* before adding the suffixes *-ed*, *-er*, *-es*, or *-est* (*pony/pon<u>ies</u>*).
- When adding the suffix *-ing*, the *y* must remain because the *i* in *-ing* does not have the sound of *i* (*satisfy/satisfy<u>ing</u>*); the *i* is part of the suffix.

The Endings *-ly* and *-y* Added as a Suffix

- The ending *-ly* can be a suffix. It changes an *adjective* to an *adverb* (*clear/clear<u>ly</u>*).
- The ending *-y* can be a suffix. It changes a *noun* to an *adjective* (*rain/rain<u>y</u>*).

DECODING

Prove the base word. Then rewrite the word, adding and underlining the suffix.

day   day<u>s</u>

baby   bab<u>ies</u>

dry   dry<u>ing</u>

brave   brave<u>ly</u>

A. Prove the base word. Then underline the suffix added to that word.

brave   brave<u>ly</u>   happy   happiest   dry   dries

cloud   cloudy   slow   slowly   pony   ponies

READING

Read the paragraph. Notice the words that have a suffix.

Jill slowly sat up and stopped crying. A smile slowly spread across her face. Bravely, she faced a gloomy situation. She knew I would gladly take her place if that would satisfy her problems. But, in fact, it would only result in multiplying them.

Lesson 59 — Name — Student **Workbook**

 Adding Suffixes to Words Ending in Y

APPLICATION ACTIVITIES

A. Write the base word of each word with a suffix.

1. slowly ___slow___

2. crying _____

3. bravely _____

4. gloomy _____

5. gladly _____

6. multiplying _____

B. Write the word in the blank, adding the suffix to correctly complete the sentence.

1. My nephew is the ___happiest___ baby I have ever seen. (happy)

2. My sister is _____ soccer on Saturday mornings. (play)

3. The soldier _____ headed into battle. (brave)

4. The sky became _____, and the kids hoped that it would rain. (cloud)

5. My son hid my _____ so he wouldn't have to go to school. (key)

C. (Circle) the words that have the suffix added correctly. Cross out the words that are spelled incorrectly. Then look at the first letter of each word you circled and fill in the missing letters to complete the phrase below.

(grayest)   ~~dryest~~   trying   ladyes   windy

strayes   happyer   rainy   keys   multiplyed

G r e a __ __ o __ __ !

168 **Reading**Horizons®

Student Workbook   Name   Lesson 60

Practicing Multi-Syllabic Words

Skills Review

This lesson reviews:
- Multi-syllabic words with *y* (*Friday*; *happy*; *army*; *python*)
- *Y* and bridges (*cyclone*; *gypsy*; *icy*; *gyrate*)
- Adjacent vowels (*contain*; *appeal*; *approach*)
- Silent *e* (*complete*; *female*; *athlete*; *conclude*)
- Digraphs, Murmur Diphthongs, and Special Vowel Sounds (*arthritis*; *understand*; *employment*)
- Nonsense words (**rizzonite*; **croistanter*)

DECODING

Divide multi-syllabic words according to the skills you have learned.

A. Prove these words.

Y in Multi-Syllabic Words

army   Friday   happy   typhoon

Bridges with Y in Multi-Syllabic Words

clergy   cymbal   gypsy   icy

Adjacent Vowels in Multi-Syllabic Words

appeal   contain   indeed   retain

Silent E in Multi-Syllabic Words

athlete   invite   decline   hibernate

Digraphs, Special Vowel Sounds, Blends, Murmur Diphthongs, and Bridges

description   boomerang

excellent   arthritis

Nonsense Words

*brouclenter   *sibtation

Lesson 60 — Practicing Multi-Syllabic Words

APPLICATION ACTIVITIES

A. Match the word with the correct definition.

typhoon — leaders in a church

hibernate — to keep

clergy — an explanation or details about something

description — a very strong tropical storm

retain — when animals sleep for an extended period of time (usually in winter)

B. Use the words and definitions from Activity A above to complete the crossword puzzle.

Across
2. when animals sleep for an extended period of time (usually in winter)
4. to keep

Down
1. an explanation or details about something
3. leaders in a church
5. a very strong tropical storm

Reading in Context

Practice reading this prescription using all the skills you've learned in Chapter 5. Review the words that are difficult for you. Then read the prescription to a teacher or friend.

FORD Pharmacy *We Care!*

Ford Pharmacy
1272 North Moonbeam Drive
Portland, OR 99025

FOR: Shauna Brown
143 Churchill Street
Portland, OR 99023

Doctor: Wheelwright
Drug: ampicillin 250mg
Quantity: 100

Date: 12/22/2010

Total: $42.33

Instructions for Use:
1. Take twice daily.
2. Take between meals, without food.
3. Take all of the pills, even if you start to feel better.
4. Possible side effects include rashes, itching, tension in the chest, difficulty breathing, or loss of vision. If you contract any of these symptoms, call your doctor.

Four refills before 6/22/2011

Batch 0467

Reading in Context

Practice reading this newspaper article using all the skills you've learned in Chapter 5. Review the words that are difficult for you. Then read the article to a teacher or friend.

TAX SCAM:
BOGUS CALL SAYS IRS LOST BANK INFO

It is now May, and the stress of taxes is past. But not for some. Last month, about six hundred people got a call like this: A man identifies himself as an IRS agent. He then claims that the person's tax forms were lost in the mail and that he or she needs to send in an additional form. As a consequence, he says that the person's tax return will be delayed. He then asks for the person's contact and bank account information in order to fill out the form over the phone and speed up the process. The result? When the victims got their bank statements in the mail, they were shocked to find that their accounts were empty. They soon called authorities.

This phony IRS agent has mainly targeted the elderly. Jack Snow, 70, from Squirrel Hill, PA, wishes he hadn't answered the phone on April 20. He lost three thousand dollars. "I've been thrifty all my life, and now this!" He says it will be harder for him to get his prescriptions. He frowns, "My arthritis is getting worse!"

The IRS claims that they have not lost any information. They want to put a quick end to the calls. If anyone calls you and asks for your bank information, hang up and call 1-800-555-3676 or 1-800-555-4484 or go to www.irs.gov. Click on the link for scams.

TAX SCAM ROUNDUP:
COPS ARREST SUSPECT

Thanks to your calls and tips, the IRS has identified a suspect in last April's tax scam. On Thursday at 2:15, Milwaukee law enforcement agents apprehended Saul White outside his Lake Forest suburban townhome. Captain Lance Knight recorded a number of the con artist's calls and says that Mr. White's voice matches the voice on the recordings.

Mr. White denies all accusations. He has hired the firm of Peterson & Stone to handle the lawsuit. His lawyer, Leroy Hatch, states that Mr. White "deplores the exploitation of innocent people."

To date, victims have lost over eight hundred thousand dollars in the scheme.

Student **Workbook** Name

Lesson 61

Decoding Exceptions

Skills Review
- Some multi-syllabic words will not follow the decoding skills. For correct pronunciation of these words, a vowel change needs to take place.
- Long vowels can be changed to short vowels but never the reverse.
- In multi-syllabic words, always divide after the *x*, even if it is not immediately followed by a consonant (*ex-it*).

DECODING

Follow the decoding skills for syllabication. If the vowel sound should be short, simply make a short vowel mark above the long vowel mark.

robin   cabin

Always divide after the *x* in multi-syllabic words that contain *x* in the first syllable, even if the *x* is not immediately followed by a consonant.

exit   exact

A. Prove these exception words.

river	seven	solid	punish	exam
finish	study	exist	credit	copy

READING

Read this story. Notice the words that are decoding exceptions.

The first shadow of evening fell over the cabin. It was already beginning to cool off. By night, it would be frigid! A shiver ran down my spine, and I pulled my coat around me. It was my habit to visit the cabin whenever I was working on a novel. The setting holds some sort of magic. It helps me to find the exact words I'm looking for. Maybe it is the sound of the river or the lavish mountain wildflowers. But while I'm here, I always manage to finish my work with a clever ending.

Lesson 61 Name — Student **Workbook**

Decoding Exceptions

APPLICATION ACTIVITIES

A. Circle the words in the sentences from the story that are decoding exceptions.

1. The first shadow of the evening fell over the cabin.
2. By night, it would be frigid!
3. A shiver ran down my spine, and I pulled my coat around me.
4. It was my habit to visit the cabin whenever I was working on a novel.
5. The setting holds some sort of magic.

B. Match the word with the correct definition. Draw a line from the word on the left to the definition on the right.

1. frigid   extravagant; generous

2. shiver   to shake or tremble from cold or fear

3. magic   very cold in temperature

4. lavish   illusions; special enchanting power

C. Unscramble the words to make real words that are decoding exceptions.

1. nmole _____   4. gadron _____

2. tidcre _____   5. itisv   _____

3. dsoli   _____

D. Circle the sound of the vowel in the syllable that is underlined.

1. r<u>a</u>pid   (ă)   ā   ə   6. n<u>e</u>ver   ĕ   ē   ə
2. b<u>a</u>by   ă   ā   ə   7. m<u>e</u>thod ĕ   ē   ə
3. s<u>a</u>lad   ă   ā   ə   8. <u>e</u>xam   ĕ   ē   ə
4. <u>a</u>round ă   ā   ə   9. h<u>y</u>per   ĭ   ī   ə
5. c<u>e</u>dar   ĕ   ē   ə   10. c<u>i</u>vil   ĭ   ī   ə

Student **Workbook**   Name

Double Consonants and -KE, -CK, -K, and -C

Skills Review

- Double consonants: When double consonants come in a word, the first of the two double consonants is usually not pronounced (di*nn*er, bo*nn*et).
- Double c: When the vowels *a*, *o*, or *u* follow the double c, only one sound for c is heard, /k/ (a*cc*ount; a*cc*ord). When the vowels *i* or *e* follow the double c, two sounds for c are heard, /ks/, due to the bridge *s* (a*cc*ent; a*cc*ess).
- Long vowel, silent e words end in -ke (ba*ke*; hi*ke*).
- If the vowel is short and no other guardian consonant is heard in a single-syllable word, the spelling is -ck (ba*ck*; de*ck*).
- Words that end in /k/ and are preceded by adjacent vowels, Murmur Diphthongs, Special Vowel Sounds, and the *nk* Special Vowel Combination, and words that have *l* as an additional guardian consonant will end in k in single-syllable words (spea*k*; spar*k*; boo*k*; hun*k*; mil*k*).
- When /k/ is heard in the middle of a word, the spelling is c (dedu*c*t; lo*c*ate). Exceptions: napkin; monkey; donkey.
- Multi-syllabic words end in the spelling of c (picni*c*; traffi*c*). Exception: attack.

DECODING

Double Consonants

There are no special markings for double consonants. You can mark the first double consonant silent to help you remember that it is not pronounced.

Use a bridge *s* in words where the second c is followed by an *i* or *e*.

Spelling with -ke, -ck, -k, and -c

When using ck, remember it is marked as a Digraph.

A. Prove these words.

acclaim   happy   hike   accent

stuck   frantic   spark   traffic

Lesson 62 — Name _____ — Student **Workbook**

Double Consonants and -KE, -CK, -K, and -C

APPLICATION ACTIVITIES

A. If the double *c* in the word makes one sound, /k/, write the word in the first column ("/k/"). If the double *c* makes two sounds, /ks/, write the word in the second column ("/ks/"). (Letters between "/ /" represent sounds.

~~accede~~   accomplish
account   accommodate
accept   accident
access   acclaim

/k/	/ks/
	accede

B. Look at the vowel. Determine whether you should use a -ke, -ck, -c, or -k to complete the word. Write the correct word ending in the space provided.

1. haw___
2. ōa___
3. for___
4. jō___
5. mil___
6. tā___
7. loo___
8. spēa___
9. trun___
10. panĭ___
11. dŭ___
12. bar___
13. rŏ___
14. musĭ___
15. Pacifĭ___

Student **Workbook** Name

MCW 13

Most Common Words List 13

Skills Review
- Most Common Words are words that are used often when reading and sometimes do not follow phonetic skills.

Most Common Words List 13

| weight | brother | gone | buy | floor | view |
| lose | guess | shoe | woman | women | |

A. Read the story. Circle the Most Common Words from List 13.

My brother met a woman on the dance floor last week, and I guess he really likes her! In fact, he has a date with her tonight. He has gone to the store to buy new clothes, and he polished his shoe where he had a scuff mark. And now he wants to lose weight! He has never cared about doing these kinds of things for other women he's dated in the past. Maybe he's changed his point of view about needing to take better care of himself!

B. One of the words in each set is a Most Common Word, and the other is a nonsense word. Circle the Most Common Word.

Example: (buy) ybu

1. floor	frool	7. gone	gnoe
2. esoh	shoe	8. seugs	guess
3. wevi	view	9. lose	sloe
4. woman	monaw	10. yub	buy
5. rethrbo	brother	11. mowen	women
6. wigeth	weight		

ReadingHorizons®   177

Most Common Words List 13

C. Circle the Most Common Word to complete each sentence. Use the sentence as a clue. Then write the word on the line.

Example: kopw**buy**athre (I need to go to the store to _buy_ food.)

1. weight krel (My brother wants to lose _____.)

2. mlw brother h (My _____ wants to lose weight.)

3. gone skel (He has _____ to the store.)

4. gl in buy (He went to the store to _____ some new clothes.)

5. gl floor pe (He met her on the dance _____.)

6. vmep view (He has changed his point of _____.)

7. nas lose i (He wants to _____ weight.)

8. veks guess (I _____ he really likes her.)

9. shoe me op (He polished his _____.)

10. fer woman b (He met a _____ on the dance floor.)

11. kr women me (He has not done that for other _____.)

Student Workbook

Lesson 63

Letter Combinations That Split

Skills Review
- Some blends will split in multi-syllabic words, including *sc*, *sk*, *sp*, and *st* (*mas-cot*; *bas-ket*; *whis-per*; *sis-ter*).
- The Digraph *gn* will split if it comes in the middle of a word (*sig-nal*; *ig-nore*).
- Special Vowel Combinations often split when they are in the middle of multi-syllabic words. The vowel in the *-ng* or *-nk* Special Vowel Combination usually keeps the same sound it had in the Special Vowel Combination (*an-ger*; *sin-gle*). Vowels in the *-ll* Special Vowel Combinations are usually short.
- Context is needed to know when letter combinations split.

DECODING

Blends or Digraphs That Split
Decode the word, marking the Blend or Digraph with an arc underneath. Then split between the Blend or Digraph.

Special Vowel Combinations That Split
If the vowel keeps the sound of the Special Vowel Combination, keep the Special Vowel Combination marked with an arc even though it's divided to remind you to pronounce the word with the Special Vowel Combination sound.

If the vowel sound in a Special Vowel Combination becomes short, remove the arc, and mark the vowel short.

A. Prove the following words.

basket   discuss   cognate   disposal

mister   history   gasket   ignore

READING

Read the story. Notice the words that contain letter combinations that split.

    James positioned himself behind a large clump of oak brush. Being certain he could not be seen, he watched as his older sister, escorted by Mr. Elkins, spread her yellow blanket, tossed out some comfortable pillows,

Lesson 63 — Name — Student **Workbook**

Letter Combinations That Split

and set out a plastic picnic basket filled with food. The prospect of Mr. Elkins asking out his sister had never occurred to James. Mr. Elkins was the new history professor. James had not even known he was single, but now he could not ignore the fact that if this relationship with his sister should ignite, he was sure to do better in history class!

APPLICATION ACTIVITIES

A. Use the words with letter combinations that split from the reading passage above to complete the sentences.

1. His sister had a _____ picnic basket.

2. Mr. Elkins was the new _____ professor.

3. James could not _____ the fact that if this relationship went well, he would do better in history class.

B. (Circle) the word that matches the definition.

1. To pay no attention.

    ignore   signet   misplace

2. A title of respect for a man.

    disturb   mister   cognate

3. To exchange ideas by talking with another person or group.

    disposal   discuss   basket

C. (Circle) the words in which the Digraph or Blend will split.

include	(mistake)	inflate	disturb
express	blister	system	instrument
transpire	disposal	represent	staple

Student **Workbook**   Name

Lesson 64

Spelling with -SS, -CE, or -SE

Skills Review

- One-syllable, *short vowel* words ending in the /s/ sound usually end in *ss* (cla*ss*; dre*ss*).
- One-syllable, *long vowel* words ending in the /s/ sound are usually spelled with *ce* (fa*ce*; ni*ce*). Some exceptions: ba*se*; ca*se*; cha*se*; va*se*.
- Most one-syllable, *short vowel* words with a *consonant* followed by the /s/ sound at the end are spelled with *ce* (dan*ce*; fen*ce*).
- Some one-syllable words containing *adjacent vowels*, *Murmur Diphthongs*, and *Special Vowel Sounds* end in *se* (gee*se*; hor*se*; blou*se*). However, some words containing the same vowel sounds end in *ce* (pea*ce*, for*ce*, oun*ce*).
- Most words ending with the *se* spelling have the /z/ sound (plea*se*; surpri*se*).

DECODING

There are no special markings for these endings. Prove the word according to the skills you know.

miss   trace

If a word that ends in *se* is pronounced /z/, you can put a small *z* above the *s* to remind you of the pronunciation.

please   surprise

A. Prove these words.

choice   class   fence   rice

peace   spice   cheese   kiss

APPLICATION ACTIVITIES

A. Circle the words that end in the /s/ sound. Underline the words that end in the /z/ sound.

<u>surprise</u>      please   ounce

cheese   glass   geese   case

trace   because   fence   prince

Lesson 64 Name Student **Workbook**

Spelling with -SS, -CE, or -SE

B. Use the words from the box to complete the poem. Not all of the words will be used.

course	race	class	pace
surpass	face	horse	nice

My friend Nikki likes to run,
So she decided to enter a _____.
She asked if I would time her,   1.
And she kept an excellent _____.
                                          2.

She ran almost every day,
And still took her aerobics _____.
Her speed kept increasing,   3.
There was no one who could _____.
                                          4.

The day for the race came,
She was ready for the _____.
There is no way she could have been faster,   5.
Unless she was riding a _____!
                                          6.

C. All but one of the Blends or consonants can create a new word ending in either *ss, ce,* or *se*. Cross out the Blend or consonant that would NOT create a real word. Then write the new words on the lines.

Example: ___ance: d-   tr-   ~~bt-~~   Fr-
         New words: _dance_   _trance_   _France_

1. ___ace: sp-   tr-   l-   sm-

   New words: _____ _____ _____

2. ___ice: m-   tw-   f-   r-

   New words: _____ _____ _____

3. ___ess: dr-   cl-   bl-   pr-

   New words: _____ _____ _____

4. ___ouse: bl-   m-   sp-   sn-

   New words: _____ _____ _____

Student **Workbook** Name Lesson 65

Sounds of *EU* and *EW*

Skills Review
- *Eu* and *ew* each have *two* sounds. They can both have the sounds of long *u* (as in *feud* and *few*) and /oo/ (as in *neutral* and *new*).
- *Eu* is not used at the end of a word, but *ew* is.

DECODING

Although this vowel combination is not a Special Vowel Sound, it is marked the same. Put an *x* underneath and between the *eu* or *ew*, and draw an arc underneath.

new feud
 x   x

A. Prove these words.

chew   sleuth   few   feud

feudal   curfew   mildew   neutral

APPLICATION ACTIVITIES

A. Circle the word that matches the definition.

1. detective

    grew   few   sleuth

2. to make like new

    knew   renew   curfew

3. benches used in a church

    pew   drew   pewter

4. a speech or writing in honor of someone who has died

    neutron   eulogy   deuce

5. a quarrel or fight that sometimes lasts a long time

    threw   sewer   feud

Sounds of EU and EW

B. Unscramble the words with the combinations *eu* and *ew* to make real words. Use the words in the box as clues. (Four of the words in the box are the answers.)

screw	sleuth	sewer	chew	drew
jewel	blew	threw	nephew	neutral

1. reews   (s) _c_ _r_ _e_ _w_

2. welb   _b_ _l_ (e) _w_

3. hcwe   _c_ _h_ (e) _w_

4. ewrth   (t) _h_ _r_ _e_ _w_

C. Take the letters in the circles and unscramble them to answer the question below.

What can be a type of soup with meat and vegetables and also mean to worry or get excited about something?

Answer: _____

Student Workbook Name _____

Lesson 66

Vowels That Reverse

Skills Review
- Four adjacent vowels and two Special Vowel Sounds can reverse in spelling.
- The four adjacent vowels that reverse are *ai/ia*, *oe/eo*, *oa/ao*, and *ui/iu* (p*ia*no; n*eo*n; ch*ao*s; stad*iu*m).
- The two Special Vowel Sounds that reverse are *au/ua* and *oi/io* (tr*ua*nt; rad*io*).
- Each vowel will be sounded and will form a syllable.

DECODING

When both sounds are heard, place a dot under each vowel that is reversed rather than an *x*. Once marked, they no longer work as adjacent vowels. There is a vowel sound for each syllable.

A. Prove the following words.

| video | aorta | diagram | medium |

| dual | lion | trial | stadium |

APPLICATION ACTIVITIES

A. Circle the correct sound that the underlined vowel makes.

1. appl*i*ance   ī   ē   ə

2. rod*e*o   ĕ   ē   ə

3. ch*a*os   ā   ă   ə

4. gymnas*i*um   ī   ē   ə

5. man*u*al   /oo/ (as in zoo)   ū   ə

6. l*i*on   ī   ē   ə

Lesson 66

Name _____

Student **Workbook**

Vowels That Reverse

B. Circle the correct sound that the second adjacent (underlined) vowel makes.

1. gi<u>a</u>nt   ā   ă   ə

2. stere<u>o</u>   ō   ŏ   ə

3. Na<u>o</u>mi   ō   ŏ   ə

4. premi<u>u</u>m   ū   ŭ   /oo/ (as in zoo)

5. situ<u>a</u>te   ā   ă   ə

6. audi<u>o</u>   ō   ŏ   ə

C. Use the words from the box to complete the paragraph. Not all of the words will be used.

rodeo	casual	stadium
situate	radio	chaos

I took my kids to see the bronco riding and calf roping at the _____(1)_____. It was held in a large _____(2)_____ with lots of seating. We tried to _____(3)_____ ourselves so we could have a good view of the horses as they came out of the chute. There was a lot of noise and _____(4)_____, but it was really fun.

186

Student Workbook

Name

Lesson 67

Other Sounds of EA and IE

Skills Review

- There are *four* sounds of *ea*: long *e* (m*ea*t); short *e* (br*ea*d); long *a* (gr*ea*t; st*ea*k; br*ea*k; y*ea*); both sounds of *e* and *a* are heard (cr*ea*te; th*ea*ter). When both sounds are heard, place a *dot* under each vowel rather than an *x*.
- There are *five* sounds of *ie*: long *i* (t*ie*); *i* is silent and *e* is long (ch*ie*f); *e* comes before *i* after the consonant *c* (rece*i*ve); *ei* says long *a* (v*ei*n; w*ei*gh); both sounds of *i* and *e* are heard (d*ie*t; qu*ie*t). When both sounds are heard, place a *dot* under each vowel rather than an *x*.

DECODING

Prove words according to the sound(s) heard.

ea

long *e*: meat cream   long *a*: great break

short *e*: head deaf   both sounds are heard: create area

ie

long *i*: pie die   long *e*: chief believe

long *e* ending: brownie cookie   long *e* after *c*: receive conceit

long *a*: veil rein   long *a* before *gh*: weight sleigh

both sounds are heard: quiet audience

A. Prove these words.

field   tie   rookie   vein   dream

weigh   diet   bread   steak   perceive

READING

Read the story. Notice the words that contain other sounds of *ea* and *ie*.

   Gene couldn't conceal his pleasure as he approached Margo's Steak House. He met his friend Don here once a year, and it was always a very pleasant occasion. They would spend the afternoon talking about their health, their wealth (or lack of it), and the weather. It would be great to hear from his dear friend!

Lesson 67 — Name — Student **Workbook**

Other Sounds of EA and IE

Don sat in a corner booth, dressed in a tie and sports coat. Gene couldn't believe how well Don looked. "He must be watching his diet," Gene thought. "He doesn't look like he weighs any more than last year! I can't continue to deceive myself. I just need to rein in my appetite and be more obedient to the rules of good health if I want to achieve such results!" Gene knew he had gained eight pounds in the last month. No pie today!

APPLICATION ACTIVITIES

A. Use the reading passage above to answer the questions.

1. Where did Gene meet his friend Don? _____

2. What was one of the things they would talk about? _____

3. What did Don dress in? _____

4. What did Gene need to rein in? _____

5. How many pounds had Gene gained? _____

B. Match the word with the definition. Draw a line from the word on the left to definition on the right.

1. veil   enjoyable

2. thief   to accept as true

3. believe   willing to follow a command

4. pleasant   one who steals

5. obedient   a cloth worn to cover the head

C. Look at the underlined letters. Circle the letters that create a new word. Write the new word you create on the line provided.
   Example: **health:**   ch (w) bl   New word: __wealth__

1. <u>th</u>ief: ch   sh   bl   New word: _____

2. vei<u>l</u>:   d   st   n   New word: _____

3. <u>b</u>elieve: t   r   st   New word: _____

188 **Reading**Horizons®

Student Workbook   Name   Lesson 68

Synonyms, Antonyms, and More

Skills Review

- *Synonyms* are words that mean approximately the same thing (*super/great*).
- *Antonyms* are words that mean the opposite of each other (*hard/soft*).
- *Homonyms* are words that have the same spelling and the same sound but different meanings (*pool* [water]/*pool* [game]).
- *Homophones* are words that have the same sound, but different spellings and meanings (*sale/sail*).
- *Heteronyms* are words that have the same spelling, but different sounds and meanings (*I read that book. Will you read it to me?*).
- *Palindromes* are words that can be spelled forward and backward and look the same (*radar; mom*).

APPLICATION ACTIVITIES

A. Circle the word that is a synonym to the first word.

1. wonderful: amazing   funny   poor

2. important: absorbent   significant   correct

3. support: format   super   help

4. hilarious: abandon   funny   return

B. Write an antonym for the word after the numbers.

1. hard

    antonym: _____

2. right

    antonym: _____

3. cold

    antonym: _____

4. tall

    antonym: _____

5. weak

    antonym: _____

6. high

    antonym: _____

Synonyms, Anytonyms, and More

C. Circle the pair of words if they are homonyms. Underline the pair of words if they are homophones. Put a box around the pair of words if they are heteronyms.

fair/fair   not/knot   read/read

lone/loan   quail/quail   alter/altar

bow/bow   cellar/seller   be/bee

D. Write these words backwards. Circle the words that are palindromes.

1. radar _____
2. civic _____
3. pool _____
4. mom _____
5. step _____
6. deed _____

Practice reading this recipe using all the skills you've learned in Chapter 6. Review the words that are difficult for you. Then read the recipe to a teacher or friend.

Spinach Salad
A quick salad for a busy day

INGREDIENTS:

Salad
1/2 head lettuce, shredded
1/4 lb. spinach, torn
a few radishes, thinly sliced
1 medium white onion, sliced

Dressing
1/2 cup olive oil
1/2 cup red wine vinegar
1 TBSP basil
1 TBSP sweetener
1/2 tsp coriander
1/2 tsp salt
1/2 tsp pepper, freshly ground
squeeze of lemon juice

DIRECTIONS:
Toss salad ingredients together. Blend dressing ingredients well. Lightly coat salad with dressing. Freshen with a squeeze of lemon juice just before serving.

Serves 6.

Note: The sweetener helps to balance the bitter flavor of the spinach, radishes, and onions.

Reading in Context

Practice reading these instructions using all the skills you've learned in Chapter 6. Review the words that are difficult for you. Then read the instructions to a teacher or friend.

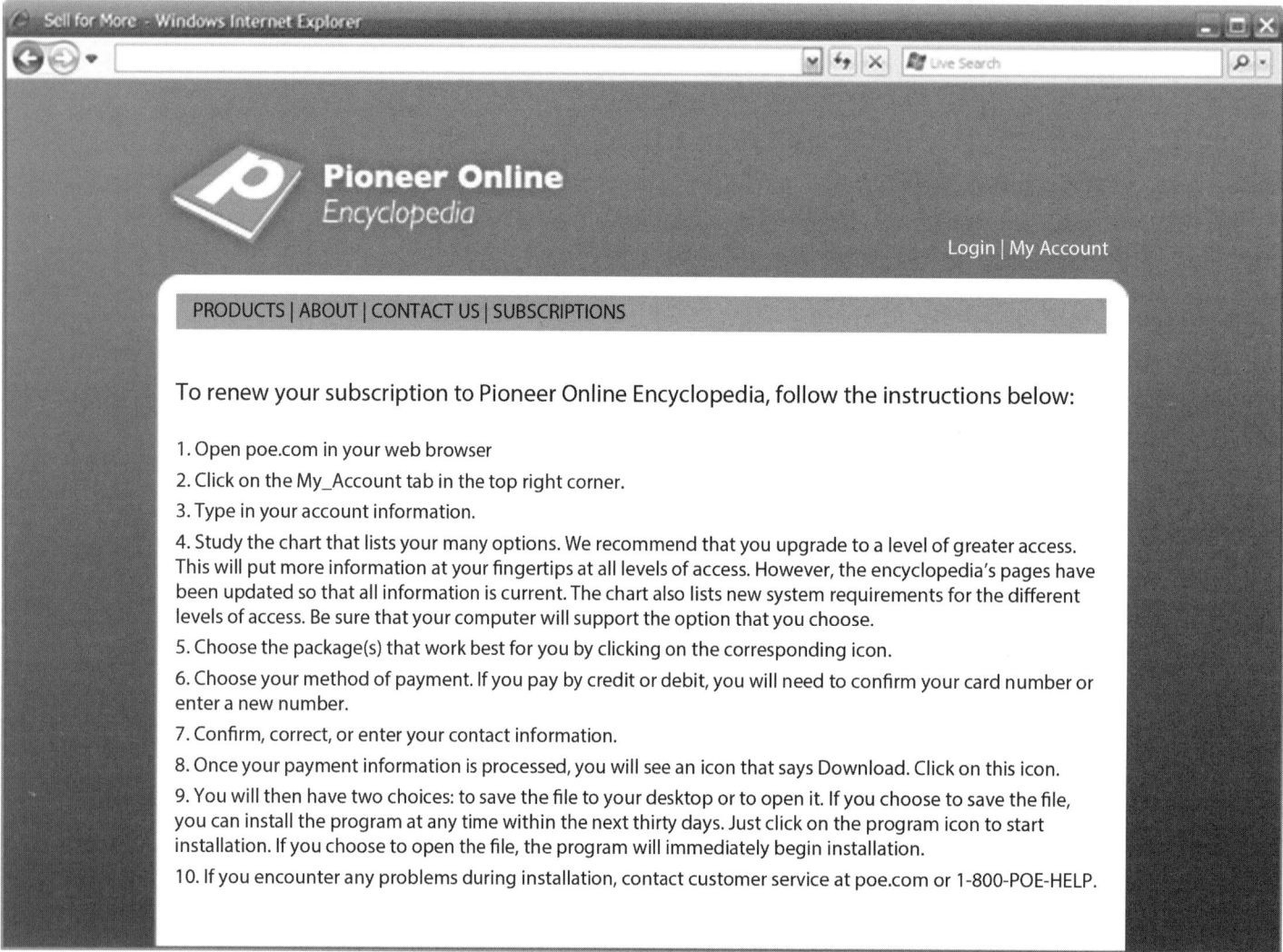

Appendix
Posters

42 Sounds

19 CONSONANTS

b c/k d f g h j l m n
p (q) r s t v w x y z

10 VOWELS

ă ĕ ŏ ŭ ĭ   ā ē ō ū ī

3 MURMUR DIPHTHONGS

ar (car) or (storm) er (her) ir (first) ur (turn)

5 DIGRAPHS   **OTHER DIGRAPHS**

ch (church) sh (shirt) wh (wheel) th (that) th (thing)   ph (f) gn kn ck wr

5 SPECIAL VOWEL SOUNDS

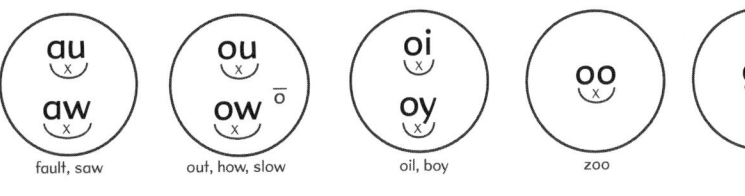

au/aw (fault, saw) ou/ow (out, how, slow) oi/oy (oil, boy) oo (zoo) oo (look)

Blends

L-BLENDS

bl cl fl gl pl sl

R-BLENDS

br cr dr fr gr pr tr

S-BLENDS

sc sk sl sm sn sp st sw

3-LETTER S-BLENDS

scr spr str spl squ

EXTRA BLENDS

dw tw

DIGRAPH BLENDS

shr thr phl (fl) phr (fr) chl (cl) chr (cr) sch (sc)

Appendix
Posters

Student Workbook

Vowels

- Aa — at
- Ee — Ed
- Oo — on
- Uu — up
- Ii — it

5 Phonetic Skills

1. sŭn*
2. hănd* *
3. gō
4. smīle
5. trāin

Posters

2 Decoding Skills

Skill 1:

bē|sīdé

prō|grăm

Skill 2:

sŭb|jĕct

ĕx|plāin

Skills 1 & 2:

ĭn|trō|dūcé

Student Workbook   Name

Appendix
Letter Formations

Practice writing the letters below.

Letter Group 1

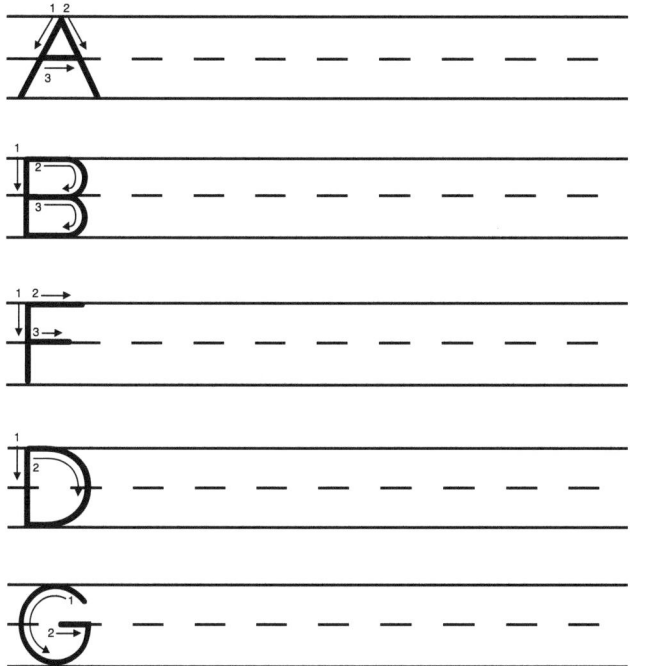
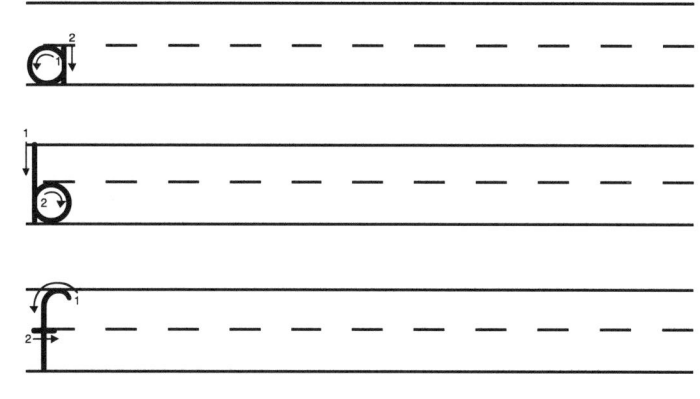
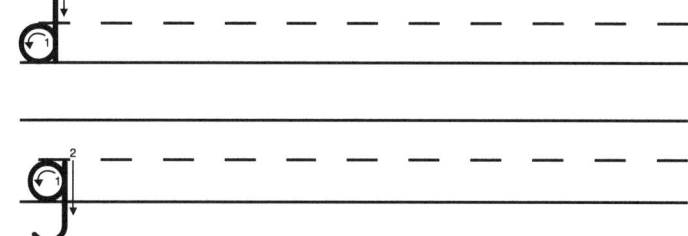

Letter Group 2

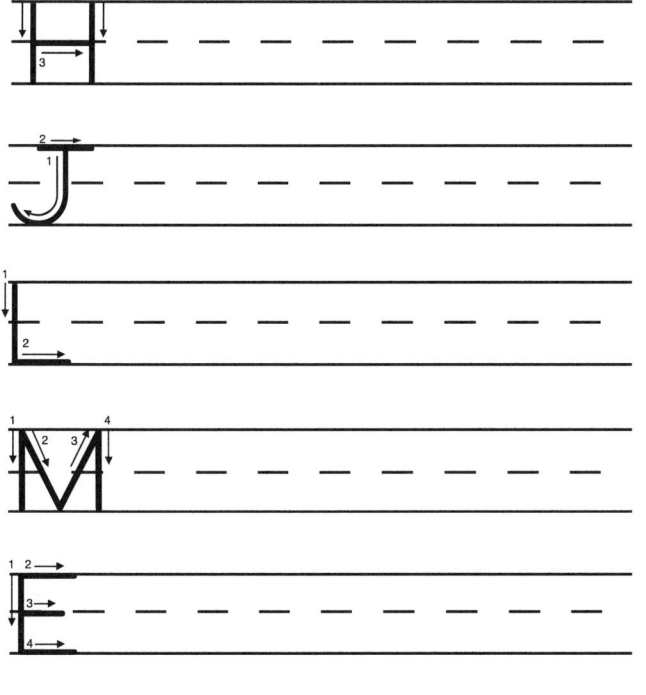
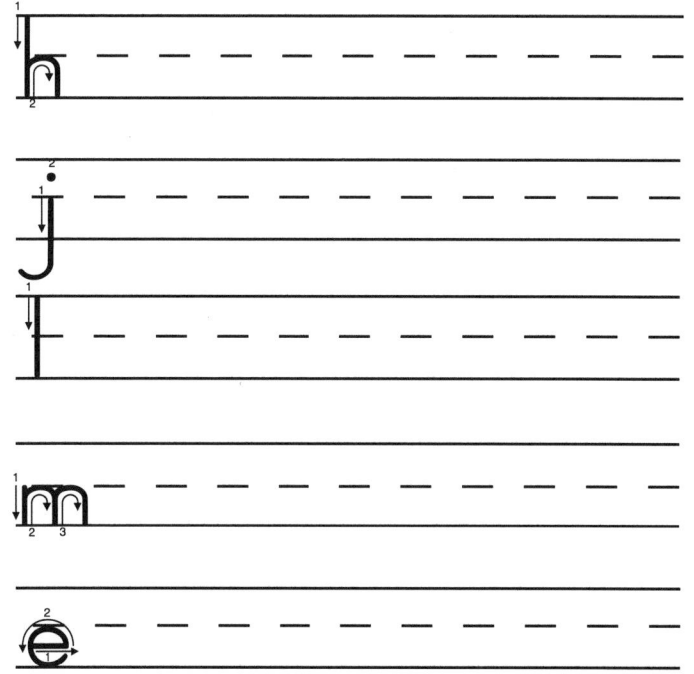

Letter Formations

Letter Group 3

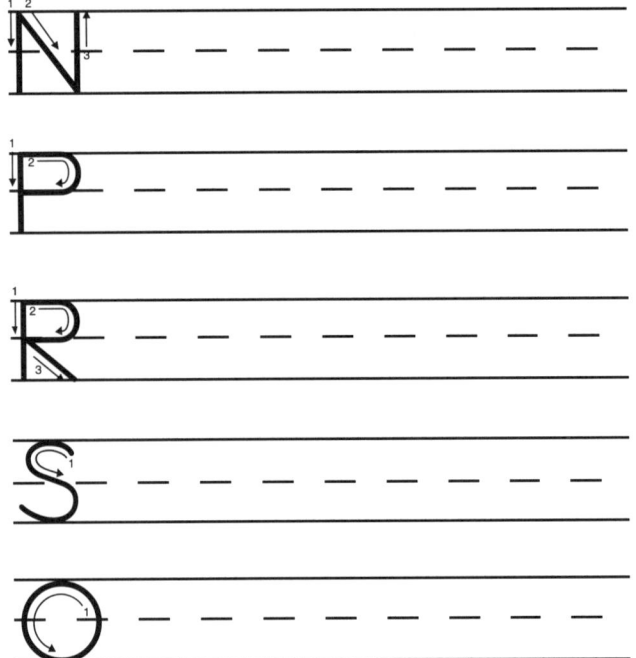
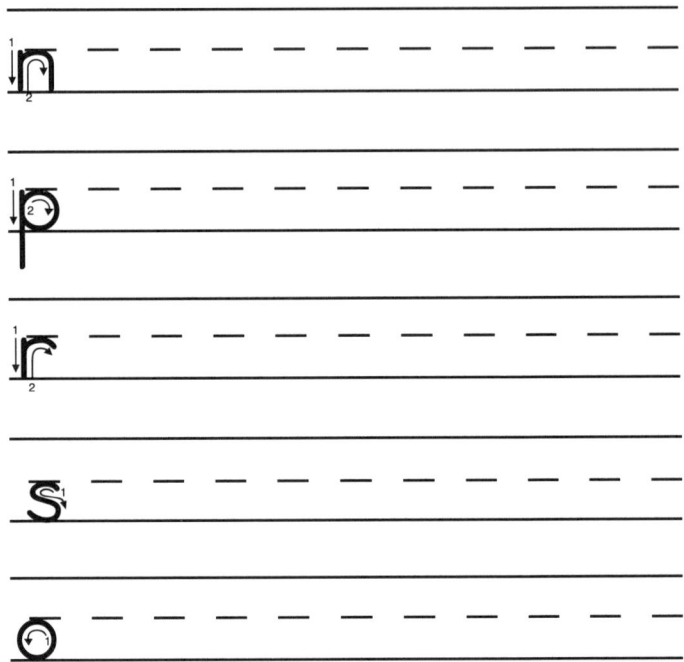

Letter Group 4

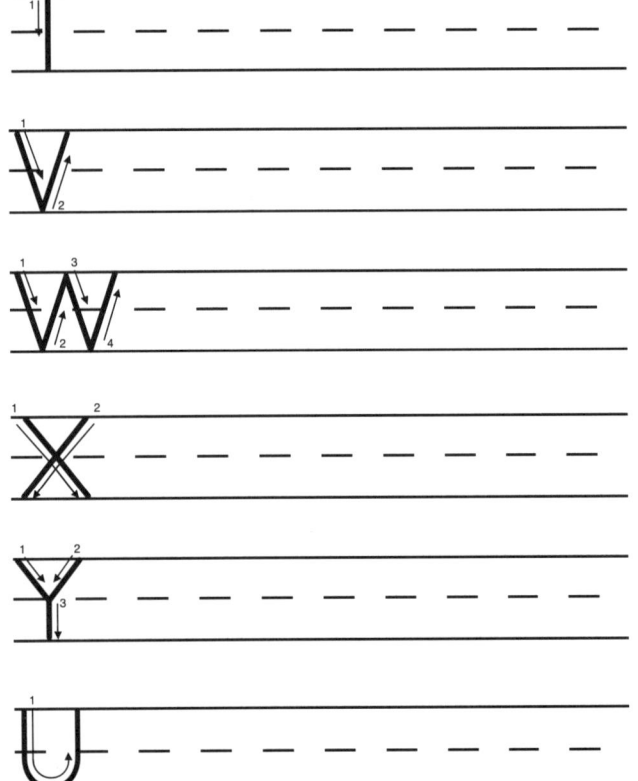
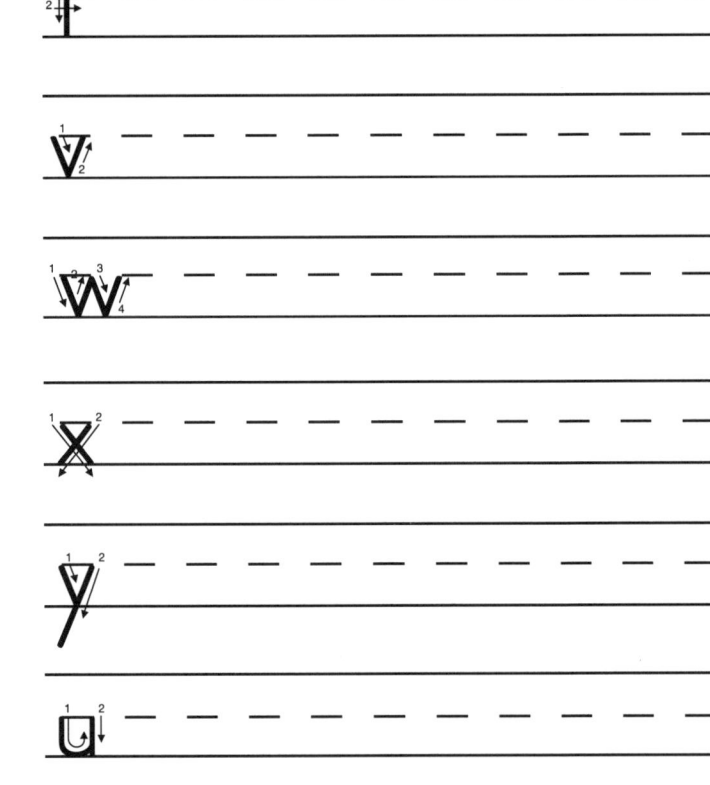

Student **Workbook** Name

Letter Formations

Letter Group 5

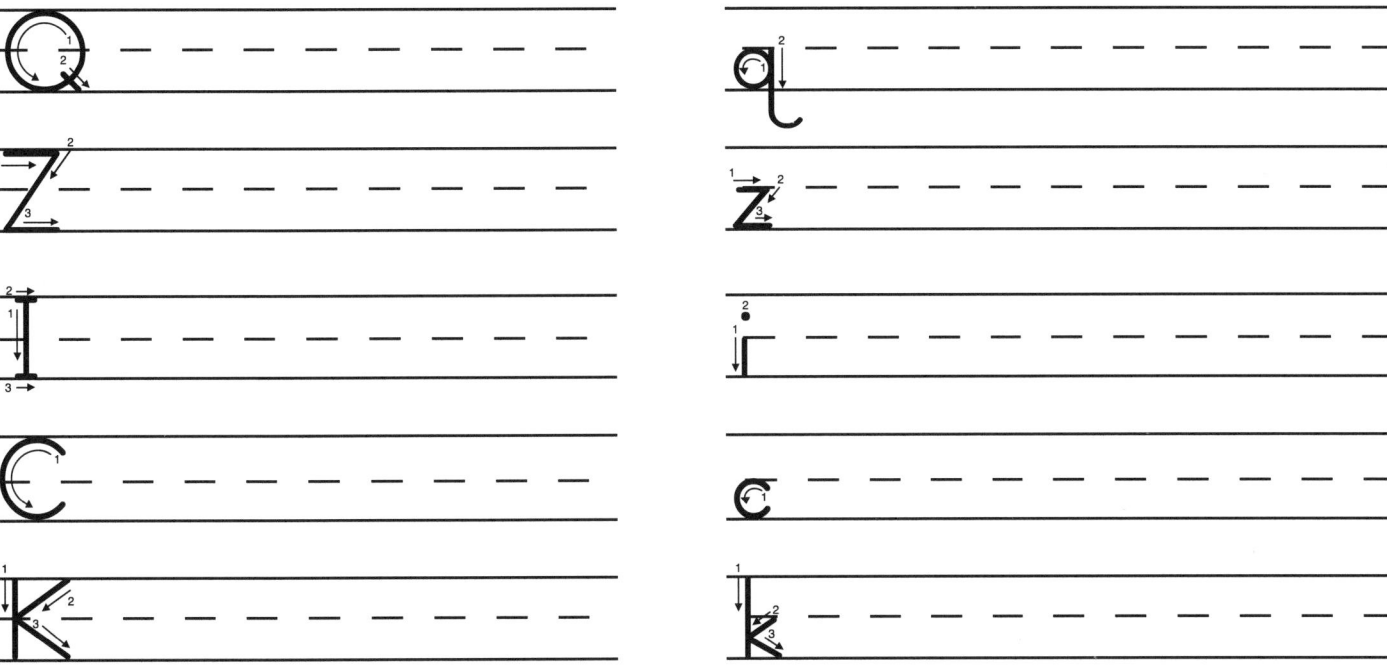

Extra Practice

Student *Workbook*

Answers

Answer Key

Lesson 1: Voiced and Voiceless (pp. 1-2)

Application Activities

B. Answers can appear in any order

Voiced	Voiceless
b	f
d	k
g	p
v	s
z	t

Lesson 2: Letter Group 1 (pp. 3-4)

Decoding

A. ba   da   fa   ga

Application Activites

A. 1. F — b
   2. B — d
   3. G — f
   4. D — g
   5. A — a

B. F ⓑ ⓐ G D ⓖ B ⓕ A ⓓ

C. Ⓑ g Ⓐ Ⓓ b Ⓕ d Ⓖ f a

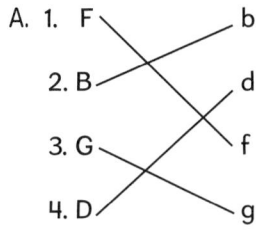

D.
- basketball — B/b
- dog — D/d
- flag — F/f
- goat — G/g
- apple — A/a

E. ⓑⓐ   af   ⓓⓐ   ag   ⓖⓐ

Lesson 3: Building Words (pp. 5-6)

Decoding

A. bad   gag   fad   gab   dad
    x   x   x   x   x

Application Activites

A. 1. bag
   2. bad
   3. dad

B. ⓑaⓖ   ⓓaⓑ   ⓖaⓓ   ⓖaⓖ
     x   x   x   x

C. 1. gag
   2. bad
   3. fab

Lesson 4: Nonsense Words (p. 7)

Decoding

A. *baf   *gaf   *daf   *bab
     x   x   x   x

Application Activites

A. bad   ⓐ*daf   dad   fad   ⓐ*bab
   ⓐ*dag   ⓐ*gaf   ⓐ*faf   ⓐ*baf   fab

B. 1. *daf
   2. *bab
   3. *faf
   4. *baf

Lesson 5: Letter Group 2 (pp. 9-10)

Decoding

A. he   be   ja   fe   je   la
   de   ma   le   me   ha   da

B. Meg   jab   led   bad   *heb   *jaf
    x   x   x   x   x   x

Application Activites

A. H   M   ⓙ   L   E   ⓗ   ⓜ   J   ⓛ   ⓔ

B. Ⓔ   h   Ⓜ   e   Ⓙ   Ⓛ   m   j   Ⓗ   l

C. 1. H — l
   2. J — e
   3. L — m
   4. M — j
   5. E — h

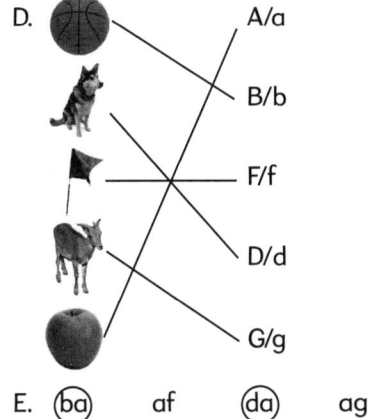
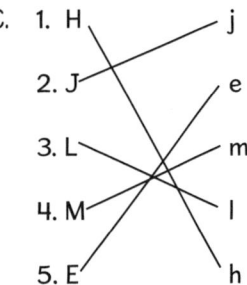

Answer Key

D.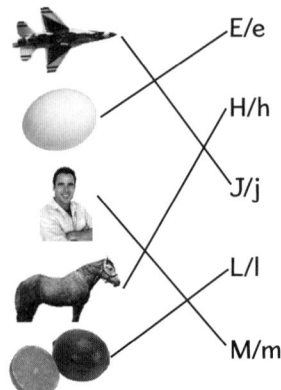

- E/e
- H/h
- J/j
- L/l
- M/m

Most Common Words List 1 (pp. 11-12)

A. 1. the   6. in   11. you
    2. that   7. it   12. a or I
    3. an   8. of   13. not
    4. I or a 9. to   14. and
    5. for   10. is

B. (I) set (an) egg (and) a ham (in) (the) pan. (It) (is) too hot. (I) go (to) (the) den.
My dog Jed (and) my cat Meg get on top (of) (the) table.
(I) go back (in) (the) kitchen.
"(That) ham (is) (not) (for) (you), Jed (and) Meg!"
(I) had (an) egg (and) (a) ham.

C. 1. (of) fo   6. eth (the)   11. (a) ta
    2. (not) tno   7. (an) na   12. yuo (you)
    3. sa (is)   8. Ih (I)   3. (and) nda
    4. (that) taht   9. ib (it)   4. ni (in)
    5. ta (to)   10. (for) ofr

D. 1. a. an b. and
    2. It
    3. to
    4. a. of b. the
    5. in
    6. a. That b. for
    7. a. I b. a
    8. is
    9. a. not b. you

Lesson 6: Sentences and Intonation (pp. 13-14)

Application Activities

A. 1. S
    2. P
    3. P
    4. S
    5. S
    6. P

B. 1. .
    2. .
    3. !
    4. ?

C. 1. ⌒
    2. ⌒
    3. ⌒
    4. ⌒
    5. ⌒
    6. ⌒

Lesson 7: Letter Group 3 (pp. 15-16)

Decoding

A. ro→ pe→ jo→ so→ lo→ ne→
    se→ ra→ no→ po→ he→ fe→

B. mop red not man *leb *hod
     x   x   x   x   x   x

Application Activities

A. N   P   R   S   O
    r   n   o   p   s
(with crossing lines matching)

B. R (s) O (p) N (r) S (o) (n) P

C. (O) p (R) s o (P) n (N) r (S)

D.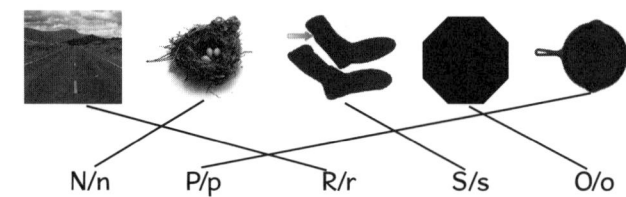

N/n   P/p   R/r   S/s   O/o

Student Workbook

Answer Key

E. 2. d; bed
    3. p; mop
    4. t; net
    5. n; man

Lesson 8: Commas (pp. 17-18)

Application Activities

A. 1. No, the ham is in the bag.
    2. Jed met Meg on May 8, 1975, in California.
    3. Is dad in the van, or is he with Jan?
    4. Do you have a ham in your bag, Meg?
    5. Dad got an egg, put it in a hot pan, and sat on the bed.
    6. Meg has a job in Sacramento, California.
    7. Don fed his hens, pups, cats, and pigs.
    8. Dad, Meg, and Jed are in the lab.

Most Common Words List 2 (pp. 19-20)

A. 1. they   8. are
    2. have   9. on
    3. this   10. at
    4. he   11. with
    5. her   12. be
    6. will   13. as
    7. we   14. but

B. (This) is my family. (We) (are) (at) the park.
    (This) is my mom and dad. (They) (have) two kids—my brother and me. The man (with) the red hat (on) is my dad. (He) is tall, (but) my mom is short.
    (This) is my mom. (Her) hat is pink.
    (This) is my brother. (He) is only ten, (but) (he) is (as) tall as my mom! (He) (will) (be) tall like my dad when (he) grows up.

C. 1. This
    2. are
    3. They
    4. with
    5. He
    6. Her
    7. have
    8. We
    9. will
    10. but
    11. on
    12. at
    13. be
    14. as

Lesson 9: Letter Group 4 (pp. 21-22)

Decoding

A. te   va   we   yu   ta   wu
    ya   vo   ye   tu   ve   vu

B. tax yam tan wax gum yes
    dug yum sun vet *fon *sab

Application Activities

A. T Y W X Y U
    v x y t u w

B. V (x) (u) Y U (w) T (y) W X (v) (t)

C. t (U) (W) v w (T) (X) y (V) (Y) u x

D. T/t   V/v   W/w   X/x   Y/y   U/u

E. 1. n; ten
    2. m; gum
    3. x; fox
    4. g; hug
    5. t; vet

Lesson 10: Letter Group 5 (pp. 23-24)

Decoding

A. co   za   ki   qui   bi   ke
    ca   que zi   mi   zo   pi

B. quip tax cut keg jig *kep
    dim   cub fix kid zap *gif

Application Activities

A. C K Q Z I
    q k i c z

ReadingHorizons® 203

Answer Key

B. ⓩ K Q ⓘ ⓒ Z C ⓚ ⓠ I

C. Ⓘ Ⓠ k i z Ⓚ Ⓒ q Ⓩ c

D.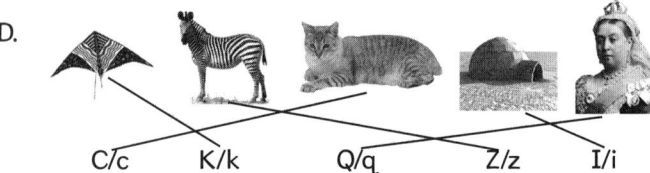
C/c   K/k   Q/q   Z/z   I/i

E. 1. keg (x under e)
   2. can (x under a)
   3. zip (x under i)

Most Common Words List 3 (pp. 25-26)

A. 1. his   6. all   11. do
   2. about   7. out   12. my
   3. from   8. me   13. was
   4. were   9. there   14. am
   5. one   10. so

B. In (my) class, (there) are (about) ten students. We are (all) (from) the U.S.

   (One) student is (from) New York. (His) name is Dan. He asked (me) what I (do) for (my) job, (so) I told him I (am) a cook.

   He (was) a cook in New York before he moved (out) here. As we talked, we found (out) that we (were) cooks at the same restaurant, just in different cities!

C. 1. epd(one)pi
   2. bd(o)mkpa
   3. tz(was)cur
   4. le(were)mip
   5. hn(all)fep
   6. (am)etmil
   7. jemp(from)t
   8. caeb(his)p
   9. nsw(my)bi
   10. (there)mrajb
   11. pr(about)gil
   12. gakm(out)c
   13. vp(me)baf
   14. wmu(so)rv

Lesson 11: Spelling with C and K (pp. 27-28)

Decoding

A. cop   kid   cat   cog   cup
   kin   cut   keg   cab   kit
(x under the vowel in each word)

Application Activities

A. 1. cap   4. cut
   2. kit   5. *kep
   3. kin   6. *cug

B. 1. can
   2. cup
   3. kid
   4. cub

Lesson 12: Direct and Indirect Quotations (pp. 29-30)

Application Activities

A. 1. I
   2. D
   3. D
   4. I
   5. D

B. 1. Jan said, "Dad and Sam went to get the map."

   2. "Your job," said Dad, "is to get this map to mom. Is that OK?"

   3. "Can I have Jan help me?" asked Sam.

   4. Dad said, "It is OK for Jan and Sam to get the map for Mom."

   5. "Your mom will be so glad," said Dad.

Most Common Words List 4 (pp. 31-32)

A. 1. would   6. look   11. go
   2. some   7. little   12. good
   3. she   8. when   13. by
   4. said   9. your   14. don't
   5. very   10. too

Student Workbook

Answer Key

B. My sister said she needs to go to the store to get some new pants. I said I would go with her to look but not to buy. I don't have very much money.

When we got to the store, I saw some pants I thought would look good, so I tried them on. They were too little. Then I saw a skirt by the pants that I liked, but my sister said, "Remember, you weren't going to buy anything? You should keep your word."

So, I didn't try it on.

C.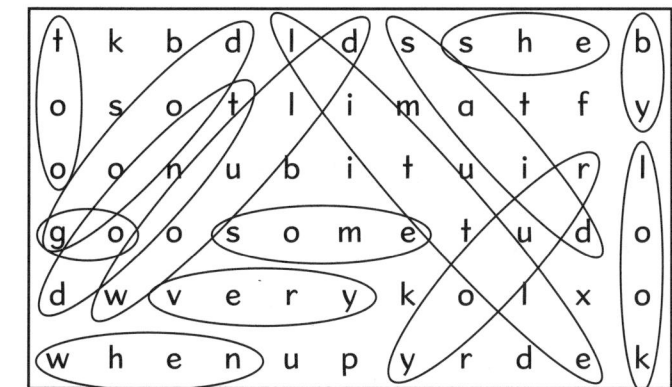

D. 1. would
2. She
3. very
4. your
5. some
6. go
7. when
8. don't
9. said
10. good
11. by
12. look
13. too
14. little

Lesson 13: Alphabetical Order (pp. 33-34)

Application Activities

A. A a B b C c D d
 E e F f G g H h
 I i J j K k L l
 M m N n O o P p

 Q q R r S s T t
 U u V v W w X x
 Y y Z z

B. 1. a, b, c, d
2. s, t, u, v
3. W, X, Y, Z
4. n, o, p, q, r
5. E, F, G, H, I
6. J, K, L M

C. 1. a) big b) fan c) hat
2. a) fog b) tan c) wax
3. a) mad b) not c) sad
4. a) box b) pit c) tag
5. a) can b) fox c) sit

Lesson 14: Articles (pp. 35-36)

Application Activities

A. 1. a 5. a 9. a 13. a
2. a 6. an 10. an 14. an
3. a 7. a 11. a 15. a
4. an 8. a 12. an 16. a

B. 1. a) A b) an
2. a) An b) a
3. a) A b) a
4. a) A b) a
5. a
6. a
7. a
8. a) an b) an

C. 1. a) The, a b) The, a
2. a) The, a b) The, a
3. a) The, an b) The, an
4. a) The, a b) The, a
5. a) The, a b) The, a

Lesson 15: L-Blends (pp. 39-40)

Decoding

A. bl cl fl gl pl sl

B. blog club flat glad plan slip

Application Activities

A. Cliff, sled, glad, flat, plans, blast

B. bl cl dl fl gl hl kl nl pl rl sl tl wl

C. 1. clip 4. slap
2. blot 5. fled
3. clam 6. slob

Answer Key

D.
clap   flag   plug   sled   black   glad

Lesson 16: Double S, F, and Z (pp. 41-42)

A. 1. s   5. z   9. f
    2. s   6. f   10. s
    3. f   7. z   11. f
    4. z   8. s   12. z

B. 1. kiss   5. buzz   9. puff
    2. class 6. cliff 10. fuss
    3. fluff 7. jazz   11. cuff
    4. fizz   8. bless 12. razz

Application Activities

A. Cliff, grass, buzz, off, fizz

B. 1. zz
   2. ff
   3. zz
   4. ff
   5. ss

C. 1. cuff
   2. miss
   3. class
   4. pass
   5. bluff
   6. razz

Lesson 17: Special Vowel Combinations: -LL, -NG, -NK (pp. 43-44)

Decoding

B. tall   wink   sing   fill   honk
   sang   well   blink full   song

Application Activities

A. Answers will vary.
   1. bull
   2. sing
   3. bank

B. 1. link, wink, blink
   2. sell, tell, swell
   3. call, fall, ball
   4. bunk, dunk, sunk
   5. rang, fang, bang
   6. sing, wing, fling

C.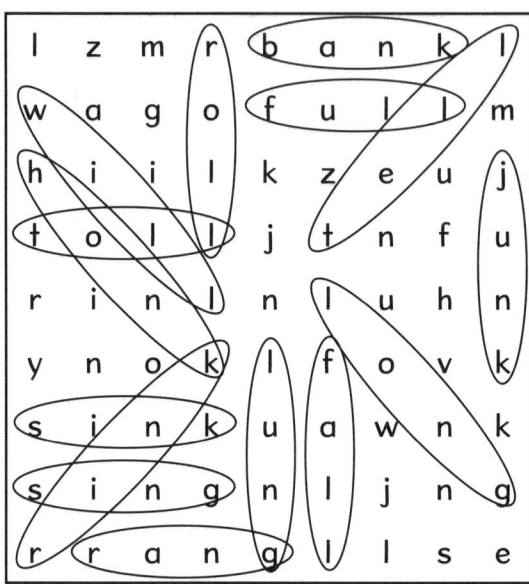

Most Common Words List 5 (pp. 45-46)

A. I know a lot of people, but I also like to meet new people every day on the bus.
   I ask people questions such as, "Where are you from?" and "What do you do?" I also ask which kinds of movies they like to go see. Then I ask how many people are in their family or if they have any kids.
   I have no problem getting into a conversation with people when I ask them things about themselves.

B. 1. know   6. any   11. then
   2. their   7. which   12. see
   3. into   8. where   13. or
   4. every   9. people   14. like
   5. when   10. no

C. 1. know
   2. see
   3. people
   4. any
   5. which
   6. then
   7. what
   8. every
   9. where
   10. or
   11. into
   12. like
   13. their
   14. no

Student Workbook — Answer Key

Lesson 18: *R*-Blends (pp. 47-48)

Decoding

A. br   cr   dr   fr   gr   pr   tr

B. bran   crop   drip   from   grab   *briff
   grip   prom   trip   drum   frog   *tran

Application Activities

A. Brad, frog, crab, drops, prods, trot

B. (br) (cr) (dr) (fr) (gr) hr kr lr nr (pr) sr (tr) vr

C. 1. grip
   2. drum
   3. bran
   4. trap
   5. crab
   6. prop

Lesson 19: Plurals (pp. 49-50)

Decoding

A. traps   classes   lids   legs
   dresses frogs   boxes cats

B. 1. claps   5. mats
   2. clams   6. glasses
   3. dogs   7. pads
   4. kisses   8. foxes

Application Activities

A. 1. her hat, cups, mats, rug, pans, and dresses

B. 1. mat
   2. cups
   3. hats
   4. rug
   5. pans
   6. dress
   7. boxes

C.

/s/	/z/	/ez/ or /iz/
hats	pens	boxes
caps	frogs	classes
cats	legs	buzzes
cuffs	pigs	dresses

Lesson 20: Possessives (pp. 51-52)

Decoding

A. dog's   Jeff's   men's   class's
   fox's   cop's   cub's   jet's

B. cats'   frogs'   pigs'   foxes'
   classes' jets'   cubs'   cops'

C. Answers can appear in any order within the column.

/s/	/z/	/ez/ or /iz/
Jeff's	dog's	class's
cop's	men's	fox's
jet's	cub's	foxes'
cats'	frogs'	classes'
jets'	pigs'	
cops'	cubs'	

Application Activities

A. 1. Tim's   2. Fred's   3. students'   4. men's

B. 1. man's job
   2. men's jobs
   3. kid's dog
   4. kids' dog
   5. class's bus
   6. classes' buses

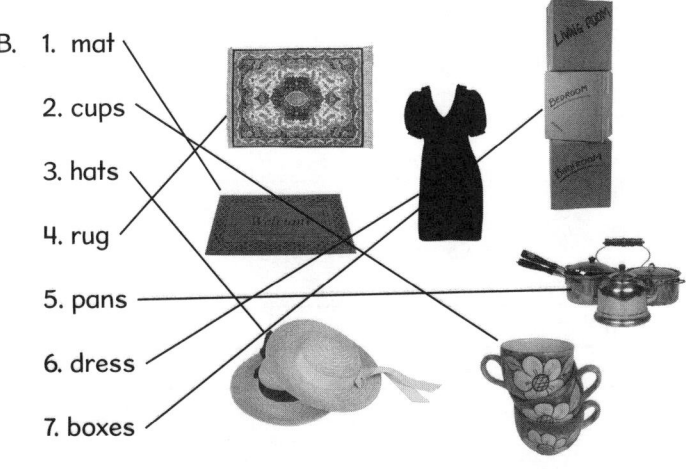

Lesson 21: *S*-Blends (pp. 53-54)

Decoding

A. sc   sk   sl   sm   sn   sp   st
   sw   scr spr str spl squ

C. scan   skin   slip   smell   squid
   snob   spill   stop   swim   task
   scrap spring strong split   clasp

Answer Key

Application Activities

A. <u>Sc</u>ot, <u>st</u>op, <u>sm</u>all, <u>sp</u>ot, <u>spr</u>ing, <u>sw</u>im, <u>sk</u>ills, <u>str</u>ong, <u>sl</u>im

B. (sc) sd (sk) (sl) (sm) (sn) (sp) sr (st) sv (sw)
   (scr) sdr sfr (spr) (str) (spl) svl (squ)

C.
1. scrap
2. spring
3. stress
4. split
5. squid
6. stop

D.
1. skin
2. scan
3. skim
4. scab
5. skid
6. scam
7. skip
8. scuff
9. scat
10. *skeb
11. *scob
12. *skizz

Lesson 22: Two Extra Blends (pp. 55-56)

Decoding

A. dw   tw

C. twin   twill   dwell   quit
   *quep   *dwip   *twed   *queb
   *dwut   twist   quill   *dwed

Application Activities

A. <u>tw</u>ists, <u>tw</u>ig, <u>tw</u>in

B. (br) bs (cl) (dr) (dw) (fr) (sc) sd (sn)
   sv (sw) sdr sfr (str) svl (squ) stw (tw)

C.
1. twin
2. dwell
3. twig
4. quill
5. twill
6. quit

D.
1. twig
2. dwell
3. twin
4. twill

E. twist

Most Common Words List 6 (pp. 57-58)

A. Every (year) I like to do something fun for my birthday. (It helps me to forget (how) old I am!)
   I have done (many) fun things in the past. Last (year) I (put) on my nice dress and (saw) a play (down) on the town.
   This (year) my family will (come) visit me. (Now) that I live in California, I (could) take (them) (around) to my favorite beaches. My mom (has) never (been) to a beach! My birthday will be even better (than) last (year)!

B.
1. put
2. them
3. around
4. year
5. many
6. been
7. how
8. than
9. has
10. now
11. come
12. could
13. saw
14. down

C.
1. down
2. many
3. year
4. has
5. around
6. saw
7. How
8. been
9. could
10. come
11. put
12. than
13. now
14. them

Lesson 23: Short and Long Vowels (pp. 61-62)

Decoding

A. ă   ĕ   ŏ   ŭ   ĭ

B. ā   ē   ō   ū   ī

Application Activities

A.
Short Vowels

ă	ĕ	ŏ	ŭ	ĭ
can	ten	off	up	kid

Student Workbook

Answer Key

Long Vowels

ā	ē	ō	ū	ī
pay	be	go	cute	mile

B. tā̃ nē kē̃ rō bū̃
   cā pō̃ mī̃ dū fī

C.
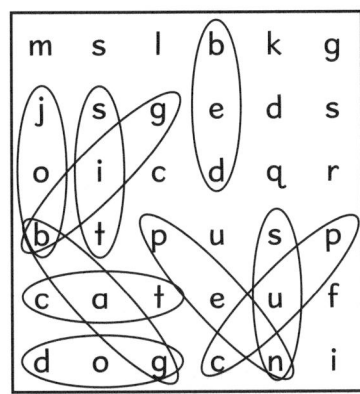

Lesson 24: Phonetic Skill 1 (pp. 63-64)

Decoding

A. hat*   bed*   rug*   kid*

B. mŏm*   bŏx*   bĭg*   stĕp*
   x   x   x   x
   rŭn*   quĭt* plăn* nŭt*
   x   x   x   x

Application Activities

A. 1. pen   4. *kep
   2. drop 5. plus
   3. cup   6. trip

B. 1. hog   4. tap
   2. men   5. hit
   3. cup   6. bad

C. 1. mad glad sad
   2. it   split hit

Lesson 25: Phonetic Skill 2 (pp. 65-66)

Decoding

A. last** help** soft** must** milk**

B. list** send** next** stand**
   x   x   x   x
   ăsk**   cŏst** dŭst** lĭft**
   x   x   x   x

Application Activities

A. Answers will vary. Answers include: spend, less, rent, help, kept, west, end, cost, best, act, fast, last, must

B. 1. fast   4. best
      past   rest
   2. dust   5. land
      just   band
   3. send   6. twist
      spend   mist

C.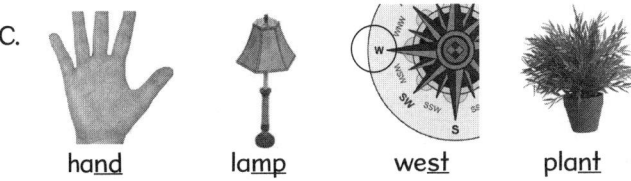

   hand   lamp   west   plant

D. Answers will vary. Sample answers include:
   Your hand has five fingers.
   The lamp was on.
   Go west when you pass the tree.
   The plant is green.

Lesson 26: Vowel Families O and I (pp. 67-68)

Decoding

A. ōld   ōlt   ōst   īnd   īld
   x   x   x   x   x

B. hōld jōlt mōst grīnd mīld
   x   x   x   x   x
   scŏld vŏlt hŏst mĭnd   wīld
   x   x   x   x   x

Application Activities

A. 1. old: mold, told, hold
   2. find: mind, kind

B. 1. gold
   2. wild
   3. kind
   4. bolt
   5. host

C. 1. volt   3. mild   5. sold
   2. mind   4. post

Answer Key

Lesson 27: Parts of Speech (pp. 69-70)

A. (hat) red (rug) (kid) (cat)
   big (bed) old (dog) small

B. 1. Ask
   2. Help
   3. spend
   4. Mix
   5. swim

C. 1. slowly
   2. softly
   3. loudly
   4. badly
   5. sadly
   6. gladly

Lesson 28: Adding Suffixes to Phonetic Skills 1 and 2 (pp. 71-72)

Decoding

A. clapping bumped lifting biggest smaller

B. 1. hit hitting   4. buzz buzzing
   2. plant planter 5. fat fattest
   3. rust rusted   6. fix fixing

Application Activities

A. 1. win   5. jump
   2. fast   6. tall
   3. strong   7. run
   4. small   8. plan

B. 1. hottest
   2. dusting
   3. camping
   4. clapped
   5. smaller

C. (flat) hunt   fix   (stop) bend
   (snag) (spit) limp   (plot) tend
   stuff   (plan) sift   (trip) (set)

Lesson 29: The Sound of -ED (pp. 73-74)

Decoding

A. mix<u>ed</u> buzz<u>ed</u> end<u>ed</u> land<u>ed</u> kiss<u>ed</u>

B. 1. beg begged   4. buzz buzzed
   2. smell smelled 5. step stepped
   3. stress stressed 6. ask asked

Application Activities

A. 1. call (d)   4. fix (t)   7. dress (t)
   2. hug (d)   5. help (t)   8. bag (d)
   3. stop (t)   6. trip (t)   9. slam (d)

B. Answers can appear in any order within each column.

/t/ (○)	/d/ (∞)	/ed/ or /id/
dropped	hugged	added
fixed	pulled	fitted
jumped	bagged	ended
stopped	buzzed	frosted
kissed	filmed	tested

Most Common Words List 7 (pp. 75-76)

A. I love to visit my grandma. She is getting old, but I (think) she is still so (much) fun. She is the (only) person (who) can make me feel so good. (After) school, I (walk) (over) to her house. When I get there, she says, "Come (here) and give me a hug!"

(Our) favorite thing to do is to play games together. We can play for (two) hours and not get tired. We (also) like to do (other) things like look at her big tree and pick fruit off (its) branches.

When I leave grandma's house, I already can't wait to go (back)!

B. 1. two   6. back   11. after
   2. much   7. our   12. its
   3. here   8. think   13. also
   4. only   9. over   14. walk
   5. who   10. other

Student Workbook — Answer Key

C. 1. (think)chlexu
2. mipg(much)pw
3. ti(who)fmoel
4. tredsc(only)j
5. (after)kgoerl
6. b(walk)xapret
7. (over)peikawl
8. matg(here)ciu
9. (two)bkempl
10. perteng(its)
11. nab(our)lemk
12. efri(also)tha
13. r(back)stidef
14. decra(other)t

Lesson 30: Phonetic Skill 3 (pp. 77-78)

Decoding

A. wē mē sō Ī bē nō
    x   x   x   x   x   x

Application Activities

A. Answers will vary.
Answers include: I, Jo, me, we, go, be, so, no

B. hĭt*   hē
   hĕlp* gō
   gŏt*   hī

C.
toe	fly	three
so	hi	we
go	I	he
no		me
		be

Lesson 31: Phonetic Skill 4 (pp. 79-80)

Decoding

A. (state) can (side) (life) man (same)
(late) plan (vote) (take) red sun

B. cūtė sāfė mākė tīmė
    x   x   x   x

drīvė rūlė hōmė nāmė
  x   x   x   x

Application Activities

A. 1. quite   5. cube
   2. tape   6. note
   3. code   7. hate
   4. tube   8. ripe

B. 1. site
   2. bite
   3. made
   4. rate
   5. hope

C.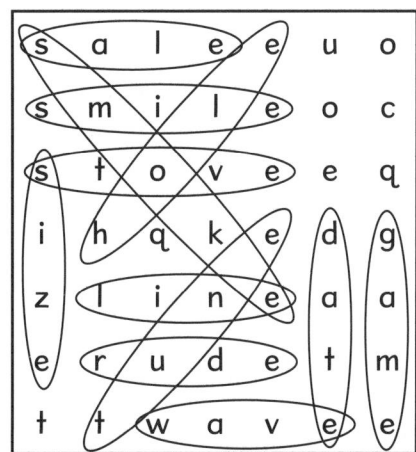

Lesson 32: Another Sound for C and G (pp. 81-82)

Decoding

A. wa͡gᵉ pla͡cᵉ gᵉl prin͡cᵉ
        j   s   j   s

B. āgė   cėll   stāgė   sĭncė*
   x j   s   x j   x s

   īcė   gėm   fācė   jŭdgė*
   x s   x j   x s   x j

Application Activities

A. 1. Roll the dice!
   2. Twice a day!
   3. Space age rides!
   4. See for a low price!

Answer Key

B. Answers will vary.
1. Answers for **-ice** include: nice, spice, rice, twice, mice, price
2. Answers for **-ace** include: space, race, brace, face, mace, place, trace, pace
3. Anwers for **-age** include: wage, rage, sage, cage, stage, page

C. Answers can appear in any order within each column.

/k/	/s/	/g/	/j/
case	cent	game	gin
deck	face	gum	huge
	lace		gist
	cite		lodge

Lesson 33: Adding Suffixes to Phonetic Skills 3 and 4 (pp. 83-84)

Decoding

A. age<u>less</u>   lik<u>ed</u>   hope<u>ful</u>   smil<u>ing</u>

B. 1. be being
    2. save saved
    3. grace graceful
    4. like likeness
    5. nice nicer
    6. late latest
    7. hope hopeless
    8. drive driveable

Application Activities

A. 1. cute, cuter
   2. date, dated
   3. hope, hopeless
   4. dance, dancer

B. 1. cute   4. fine
   2. ride   5. pride
   3. vote   6. time

C.
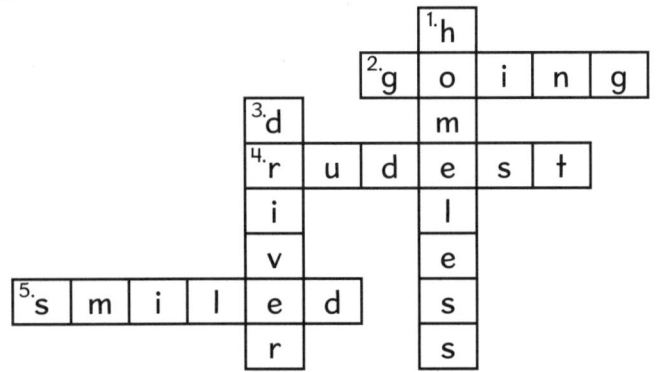

Lesson 34: Sounds of *GH*, *IGH*, and *IGHT* (pp. 85-86)

Decoding

A. bright   high   night   tight
   sigh   fight   light   flight

Application Activities

A. 1. night
   2. high
   3. rough
   4. ghost
   5. sight
   6. tough

B. (light)   ghost   tough   (might)   (right)
   (flight)   (high)   rough   (plight)   laugh
   (night)   (fight)   (bright)   (sight)   cough

C. Answers will vary.

Lesson 35: Phonetic Skill 5 and Adjacent Vowels (pp. 87-88)

Decoding

A. vote   (feel)   (true)   like   (paint) (street)
   (keep)   line   (least) (road) (read)   hope

B. need   heat   rain   say   pie
   blue   boat   toe   lie   fruit

C. Answers can appear in any order within each column.

ā	ē	ō	ū	ī
rain	need	boat	blue	pie
say	heat	toe	fruit	lie

Application Activities

A. 1. toast   4. green
   2. pea   5. beat
   3. leaf   6. train

B. 1. die   4. load
   2. meal   5. tea
   3. suit   6. seek

Student Workbook
Answer Key

C. ai   ay
    ea   ee
    oa   oe
    ui   ue
            ie

D. Answers will vary.

Lesson 36: Adding Suffixes to Phonetic Skill 5 (pp. 89-90)

Decoding

A. keep<u>ing</u>   mean<u>est</u>   paint<u>ed</u>   weak<u>er</u>

B. 1. clean cleaner
    2. deep deepest
    3. fail failed
    4. rain raining
    5. claim claimed
    6. heat heating

Application Activities

A. a) roasted b) toasted c) cleanest
   d) seated e) waiting

B. 1. sleeping
   2. gained
   3. mailed
   4. stained
   5. speeding

C. 1. seek
   2. green
   3. sweep
   4. loan
   5. boast

Most Common Words List 8 (pp. 91-92)

A. Every day, I wake up at 6:00 a.m. (First) I run (three) laps around the block. I (want) to stay fit! Then I get ready for (work).

(Before) I go to (work) I read the paper to see what is (new). On my (way) to (work) I drop my (seven)-year-old (boy) off at school.

If I feel tired, I (may) stop for a cup of tea. I (use) it to stay awake at (work). But I (never) drink tea (before) I go to bed. One time when I did that, I couldn't sleep all night. I don't (want) to do that (ever) (again).

B. 1. use   8. want
   2. before   9. never
   3. first   10. may
   4. ever   11. new
   5. seven   12. three
   6. boy   13. work
   7. way   14. again

C. 1. boy
   2. use
   3. three
   4. before
   5. again
   6. new
   7. work
   8. ever
   9. first
   10. may
   11. way
   12. seven
   13. never
   14. want

Lesson 37: Contractions (pp. 95-96)

Application Activities

A. 1. haven't   6. let's
   2. she'd   7. we'll
   3. they're   8. who've
   4. she's   9. I'm
   5. we'd   10. won't

B.
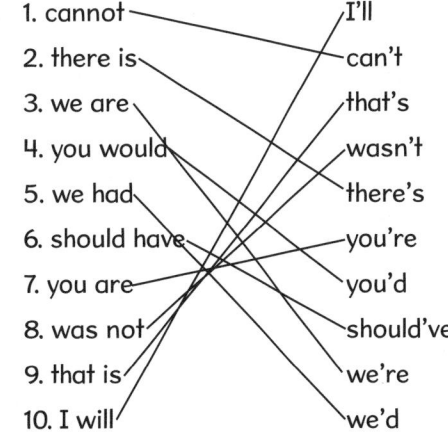

1. cannot — can't
2. there is — there's
3. we are — we're
4. you would — you'd
5. we had — we'd
6. should have — should've
7. you are — you're
8. was not — wasn't
9. that is — that's
10. I will — I'll

C. 1. should've
   2. I'll
   3. wasn't
   4. You're
   5. can't

Answer Key

Lesson 38: Many Jobs of Y (pp. 97-98)

Decoding

yĕt   yĕs   yōke   yēast
pӳx   crӳpt   Sӳd   Lӳnn
mȳ   trȳ   stȳle   bȳe
sāy   kēy   wāy   stāy

Application Activities

A. 1. spin
2. tray
3. hi
4. wipe

B. 1. a) yelled b) yelled
2. a) day b) day
3. a) style b) style
4. a) crypt b) crypt

C. [gray] (crypt) dry yum
(gym) [may] cry [pay]
(cyst) sky yell type

Lesson 39: Decoding Skill 1 (pp. 99-100)

Decoding

A. rōbŏt   bĕgin   prōvide   dēcide
delāy   behāve   nōmăd   refrāin

Application Activities

A. 1. pro — test
2. cli — max
3. re — sis
4. de — have
5. cri — cite
6. be — gree

B. 1. protest   4. degree
2. climax   5. crisis
3. recite   6. behave

C. 1. dōnāte
2. prōgrăm
3. rēcline
4. demănd
5. digĕst

D. 1. demand
2. donate

Lesson 40: Syllable Stress and the Schwa (pp. 101-102)

Decoding

A. sōfə   pĕncəl   hūmən   ēvən
stūdənt   lōcəl   mōmənt   əgrēe

B. (silənt)   (seləct)   (divīdə)   (lābəl)

Application Activities

A. 1. adult
2. evil
3. legal
4. ago
5. equal
6. private
7. adopt
8. final

B. Answers can appear in any order within each column.

1st Syllable	2nd Syllable
equal	ago
private	adult
evil	adopt
legal	
final	

Lesson 41: Last Job of Y (pp. 103-104)

Decoding

A. tīnȳ   crāzȳ   lādȳ   nāvȳ
rāinȳ   tīdȳ   hōlȳ   grēedȳ

B. replȳ   relȳ   denȳ   defȳ

Answer Key

C. Cyprus   Tyson   cyclone

Application Activities

A. 1. lazy
   2. pony
   3. lady

B.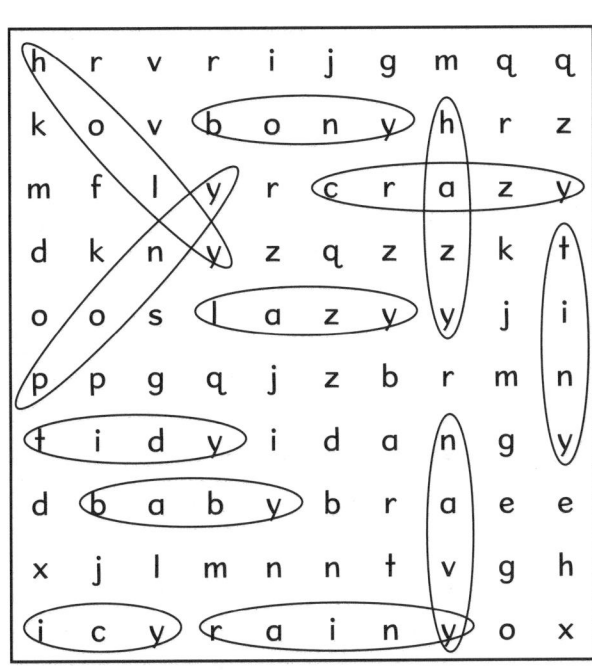

Lesson 42: Decoding Skill 2 (pp. 105-106)

Decoding

A. explain   candy   sixteen   dictate
   maintain   invite   subject   engage

Application Activities

A. 1. fifteen
   2. upset
   3. inhale
   4. console
   5. explode

B. 1. upset
   2. absent
   3. expect
   4. include
   5. complain

C. 1. complain
   2. upset
   3. include

Lesson 43: Prefixes (pp. 107-108)

Decoding

A. untie   refill   predict   dislike
   nonstop   invent   overpass   misjudge

Application Activities

A. 1. nonstop
   2. repay
   3. midsize
   4. overeat
   5. misbehave

B. 1. replay   4. retell
   2. unhappy   5. unfair
   3. unkind   6. retry

C. 2. disagree
      Prefix: dis
   3. semicircle
      Prefix: semi
   4. defrost
      Prefix: de
   5. unable
      Prefix: un

Lesson 44: -LE at the End of a Word (pp. 109-110)

Decoding

A. pickle   puzzle   cable   eagle
   simple   table   uncle   giggle

Application Activities

A. Answers will vary. Answers include:
   1. crumble, table, tumble, stable
   2. little, bottle, mantle
   3. cradle, puddle, needle

B. 1. cradle
   2. candle
   3. stable
   4. needle
   5. fiddle

Answer Key

Lesson 45: Decode Words of Any Length (pp. 111-112)

Decoding

A. independence   romantic
   equipment   absolute
   *tramsomime   concentrate

Application Activities

A. Answers can appear in any order within each column.

2 syllables	3 syllables	4 or more syllables
transit	equipment	communicate
explode	consonant	impossible
submit	cryptogram	independence
	potato	
	vitamin	
	romantic	

B. 1. No
   2. Yes
   3. Yes
   4. No
   5. No
   6. Yes

Lesson 46: Compound Words (pp. 113-114)

Decoding

A. and B.   1. pan cake
            2. sun light
            3. soft ball
            4. toe nail
            5. high way
            6. pea nut

Application Activities

A. 1. cupcakes
   2. raincoat
   3. hotdogs
   4. peanuts
   5. lipstick
   6. backpack

B. 1. week — scape
   2. air — end
   3. base — made
   4. home — time
   5. bed — ball
   6. land — plane

C. sprinkle (taillight) explode (railroad)
   (sailboat) sentence (download) jumbo
   trample (handball) rabbit (cobblestone)

Most Common Words List 9 (pp. 115-116)

A. In some places, nature looks the same all year (round). But in other places, there are (four) seasons to enjoy.
   Where I'm from, during the first (eight) months of the year, the trees are either bare or green. But in the fall, the leaves are (yellow) and (brown). The (pretty) colors last only about (four) weeks before it snows.
   (Today) I want to go on a drive (through) the forest (because) I want to see the (pretty) colors of the leaves before they go (away). It is (such) a (pretty) day for taking photos. I wish I could enjoy a drive on (more) days like (these) and take photos to give to my family so they can enjoy the (pretty) colors, too.

B. 1. today   6. yellow   11. round
   2. eight   7. four   12. brown
   3. through   8. these   13. more
   4. because   9. pretty   14. away
   5. give   10. such

C. 1. a) because
   2. b) eight
   3. a) these
   4. a) Today
   5. b) give
   6. a) more
   7. b) such
   8. a) through
   9. b) four
   10. a) away
   11. b) brown
   12. a) round
   13. b) pretty
   14. a) yellow

Student Workbook — Answer Key

Lesson 47: Murmur Diphthong AR (pp. 119-121)

Decoding

A. farm cart scar yard
   start dark card smart

B. radar artist margin garden

C. 1. barked   5. starred
    2. starting   6. scarring
    3. harder   7. farmer
    4. darkest   8. smartest

Application Activities

A. 1. Carl went to the __farm__ to help Marge.
         park (farm) card
    2. The dog began to __bark__ when Carl drove in.
         star (bark) hard
    3. Marge wore a coat and a __scarf__ around her neck.
         (scarf) tar yarn
    4. Carl parked his __car__.
         yard scar (car)
    5. Carl and Marge worked in the __garden__.
         market harvest (garden)

B. 1. car   4. bar
    2. park   5. start
    3. harp   6. yarn

C.
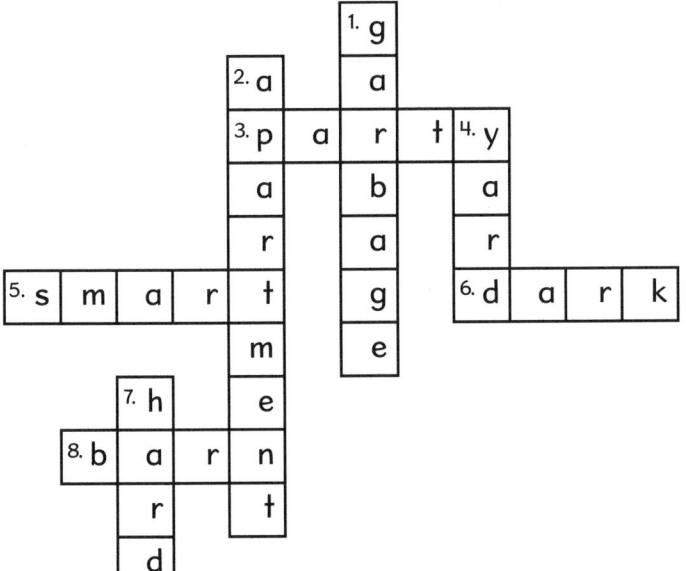

Lesson 48: Murmur Diphthong OR (pp. 123-124)

Decoding

A. storm cord born fork

B. orbit forest forgot story

C. 1. scorned   4. sorted
    2. forming   5. sporting
    3. snorted   6. corked

Application Activities

A. 1. torn, horn
    2. fork, cork
    3. lord, Ford
    4. York, stork
    5. fort, sort
    6. dorm, storm

B. 1. No
    2. Yes
    3. Yes
    4. No
    5. Yes

C.
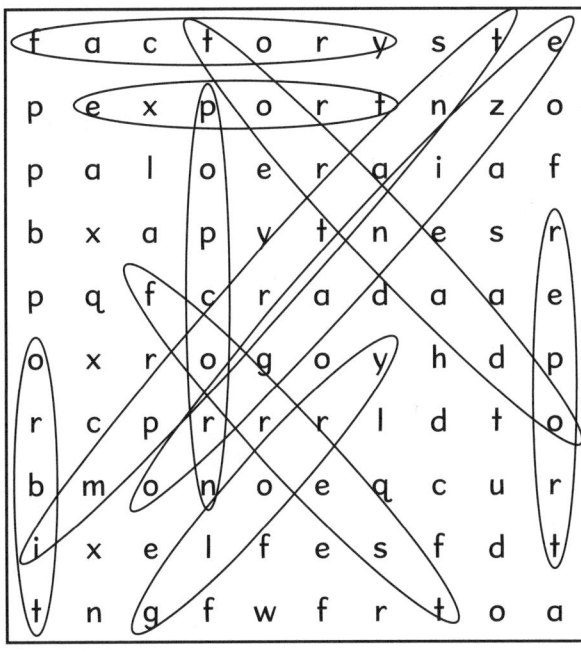

Answer Key

Lesson 49: Murmur Diphthongs ER, UR, and IR
(pp. 125-127)

Decoding

A. germ   hurt   firm   verb   curb
   clerk   skirt   first   stir   surf

B. fever   hurry   circus
   return   direct   winter

C. 1. turned   4. surfed
   2. herder   5. stirring
   3. slurring   6. firmest

Application Activities

A. 1. b) sister
   2. d) hot syrup
   3. c) a lot
   4. a) nurse
   5. a) dirt

B. 1. hurt, flirt
   2. lurk, jerk
   3. turn, concern
   4. affirm, perm
   5. stir, her
   6. purred, stirred

C. 1. meter
   2. hammer
   3. tigers
   4. sermon
   5. computer
   6. dirt

D.

Lesson 50: Exceptions to Murmur Diphthongs
(pp. 129-132)

Decoding

A. fire   large   force   curve   clear
B. heard   early
C. wand   warp   world
D. berry   parent
E. favor   major

Application Activities

A. This was by far the worst forest fire Marge had ever seen! She had been a nurse in the military and was now doing some charity work at the fire camp. She did whatever she could to help, which included serving the firefighters their meals.

A large squad of firefighters wandered into the tent for something to eat. Marge knew they would need lots of water to drink in addition to the huge quantity of hot waffles and ham the cook had made, and she hurried to serve them. They ate as if they were about to starve!

Marge listened as they spoke. She heard them say that there was some fear that their workforce was too small. They decided to warn their director of the need to hire more firefighters.

B. 1. early
   2. ferry
   3. monastery
   4. inherit
   5. warn
   6. score
   7. carve

C. 1. fire
   2. fair
   3. learn
   4. warm
   5. merry
   6. flavor

Student Workbook

Answer Key

D. Across: 3. splurged
4. fired
5. nursing
Down 1. wired
2. merging
3. staring

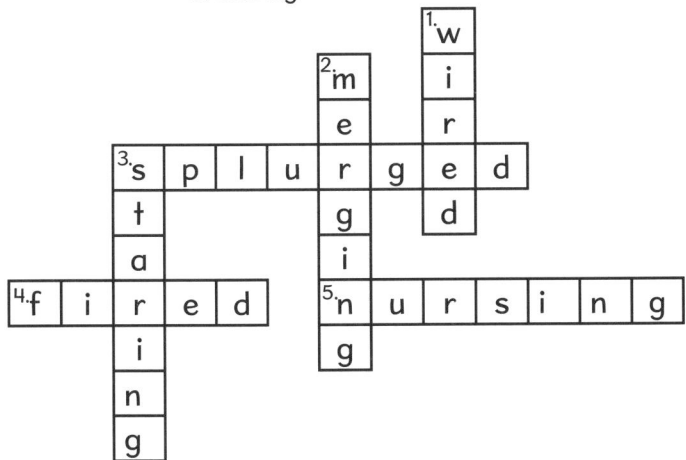

E.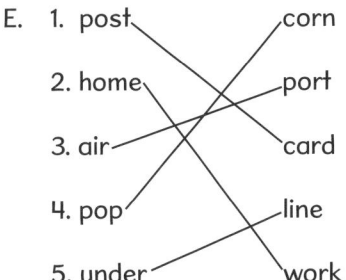
1. post — corn
2. home — port
3. air — card
4. pop — line
5. under — work

Most Common Words List 10 (pp. 133-134)

A. My (father) wants to (build) a new house on his own. The problem is he (does) not know how. He (says) the best way to (learn) is by doing. So, each Saturday he (goes) to a community class to (learn) how to (build) a house. He likes that the teacher can (answer) any of his questions.

He was having such a (great) time (learn)ing one day that he (thought) he (should) get my (mother) involved. He thinks it would be a fun project to work on (together). My (mother), on the other hand, only wants to help once they (move) into the house. She has no interest in helping to (build) the house. But she has a good (eye) for decorating!

B. Answers will vary.
1. father
2. He does not know how.
3. He goes to a community class.
4. The teacher can answer any of his questions.
5. mother

C.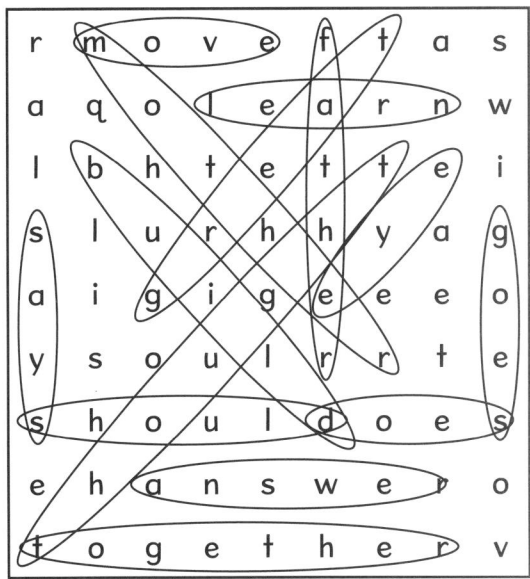

D. 1. should   8. build
    2. does   9. learn
    3. together   10. says
    4. eye   11. mother
    5. answer   12. great
    6. goes   13. thought
    7. move   14. father

Lesson 51: Digraphs CH, SH, WH, TH, and TH (pp. 135-137)

Decoding

A. beach   cash   bathe   whine   lunch
   shirt   church   thing   itch   she

B. beneath   chapter   sharpen
   whimper   athlete

C. 1. mashed   4. marched
   2. wishing   5. rancher
   3. pinched   6. coaching

Application Activities

A. 1. charm
   2. while
   3. sheets
   4. thin
   5. these

Answer Key

B. Answers will vary
1. ship
2. when
3. shin *or* chin
4. whine *or* thine
5. chop
6. wish

C. Answers can appear in any order within each column.

Voiceless (◡)	Voiced (◡)
athlete thank	mother these
math thin	this then
thirty	bother

Lesson 52: Digraphs PH, GN, KN, CK, and WR (pp. 139-142)

Decoding

A. sti**ck** kn**ee** **ph**ase **gn**a**sh** so**ck** **wr**ong assi**gn**

B. black kneel graph gnarl
   wreck knock wrist quick

C. photo pocket written
   digraph align

D. lipstick nickname checkup
   padlock payphone

Application Activities

A. 1. photos
   2. gnats
   3. knife
   4. check
   5. wrong

B. 1. The chef needed a sharp __knife__ to cut the onion.
      block (knife) pick
   2. The mechanic used a __wrench__ to fix the car.
      (wrench) knot rock
   3. Jane hung a __wreath__ on the front door for the holidays.
      lock knob (wreath)
   4. She heard a __knock__ at the door, so she went to see who it was.
      (knock) wrist gnome

C. 1. knead
   2. phony
   3. birthday
   4. homesick
   5. lipstick
   6. photograph

D. photo

Lesson 53: Digraph Blends (pp. 143-144)

Decoding

A. chrome phlox shrink throne

B. arthritis chloride shrubbery
   thrifty

Application Activities

A. Three little thrush sang their shrill song.

B. 1. throng — a large number of people crowed together
   2. thrush — a small song bird
   3. phlox — a type of plant that has flowers on it
   4. shrill — having a sharp, high sound
   5. scheme — a plan of action
   6. chrome — shiny, gray metal used on cars

C. 1. phlox
   2. chrome
   3. shrill
   4. scheme
   5. thrush

Lesson 54: Digraph Words with Plural Endings (pp. 145-146)

Decoding

A. beach**es** church**es** pitch**es** watch**es**

220

B.
1. wish — wishes
2. coach — coaches
3. ranch — ranches
4. teach — teaches
5. witch — witches
6. match — matches

Application Activities

A. 1. peaches
2. benches
3. wishes

B. hat (ash) (ranch) brick (bunch) (lunch) car (match) plate (wish)

Most Common Words List 11 (pp. 147-148)

A. My best (friend) lives 300 miles away, but we (talk) on the phone every week. We are able to (carry) on a conversation for hours. But we (both) decided to not (talk) to each other for more than an hour at a time, (though) we (always) have (enough) to (talk) about. We just have to be (sure) we don't go over our cell phone minutes. That can be expensive!

(Once) we (talked) for three hours without stopping! We lost track of time (talking) about our (young) children, our favorite (color) of paint for a bedroom, and how we weren't (sure) what to cook for dinner. Our cell phone bills cost a lot that month!

B. 1. d) her best friend
2. c) talk on the phone
3. b) false
4. c) where they go shopping
5. b) they talked for three hours
6. b) female

C. 1. talk
2. enough
3. friend
4. both
5. color
6. once
7. carry
8. young
9. always
10. sure
11. though

Lesson 55: Special Vowel Sounds AU/AW, OU/OW, OI/OY (pp. 149-152)

Decoding

A. hawk low point cow boy

B. straw blow shout moist launch

now joy vault show oil

Application Activities

A. 1. c) a house
2. a) free utilities
3. b) false
4. c) someone who wants to buy a home
5. a) someone who sells homes

B. 1. boil
2. thaw
3. pound
4. plow
5. soil
6. grow
7. hoist
8. haul

C.

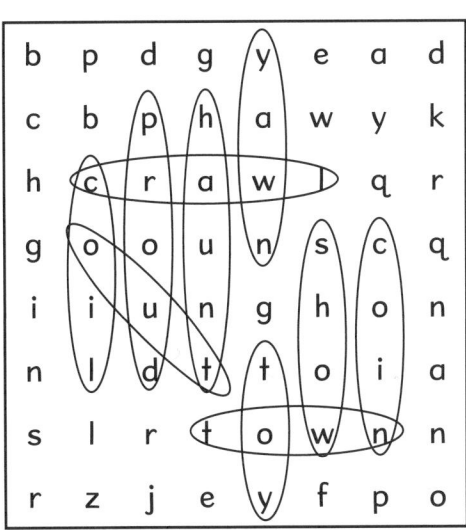

Lesson 56: Special Vowel Sounds OO and OO (pp. 153-155)

Decoding

A. book cool cook room moon

Answer Key

B. spool shook boost tooth
   spoon foot   wood   stood

Application Activities

A. Answers will vary
1. his spoon
2. on the stool at the cooking school
3. tools
4. cookbook
5. tooth

B.
1. good
2. stool
3. hook
4. foot
5. broom
6. food

C.
1. boost — to lift or raise by pushing from behind or below
2. crook — a dishonest person; thief
3. rook — a black, European crow
4. stoop — to bend head and shoulders forward and down

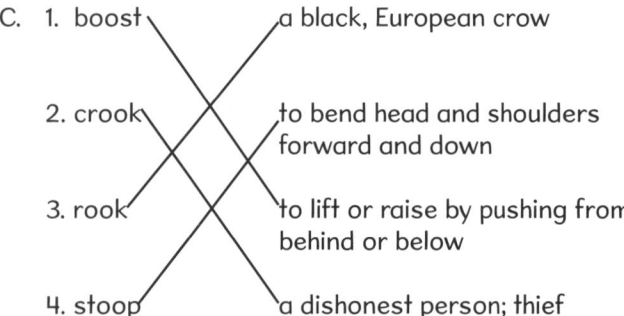

D. Answers can appear in any order within each column.

1 "zoo"			2 "look"		
pool	smooth	mood	hood	wood	hook
room	snooze	school	foot	shook	brook
tooth	spoon	troop	book	cook	stood
booth	cool	too			
tool	broom	stool			

Lesson 57: More Special Vowel Sound Skills (pp. 157-158)

Decoding

A. destroy laundry profound
   powder   bamboo   authentic
   typhoon thyroid scoundrel
   employment

B. footprint outside
   moonbeam   bookmark
   teaspoon   jawbone
   snowball   townhouse

Application Activities

A.
1. snowstorm
2. profound
3. troop
4. employment
5. downhill
6. crowning
7. jaw
8. raw
9. spoiling
10. thawing
11. broiling
12. destroy

B. (broomstick) (goodnight) cauliflower (doghouse) haunting (checkbook) (housewife) (soybean) destroy pauper (downtown) exploit (toothbrush) (playground) (rowboat)

C. Answers will vary.

Most Common Words List 12 (pp. 159-161)

A. I (love) to throw a party for my friends during the holidays even though it is a very (busy) time of year and it can cost a lot of (money) for all of the food and decorations.

One time, when I was almost finished making the preparations for a party, I (heard) a knock on the (door). Had someone arrived (early)? As I walked (toward) the (door), I realized I had (done) (nothing) to get myself ready! I was so (busy) getting the food ready for the party that I forgot about getting myself ready! Oh, well! So much for my own (beauty) at my own party! I just had to (laugh) it off.

Student Workbook — Answer Key

B.
1. done
2. nothing
3. heard
4. love
5. toward
6. busy
7. early
8. laugh
9. money
10. beauty
11. door

C.
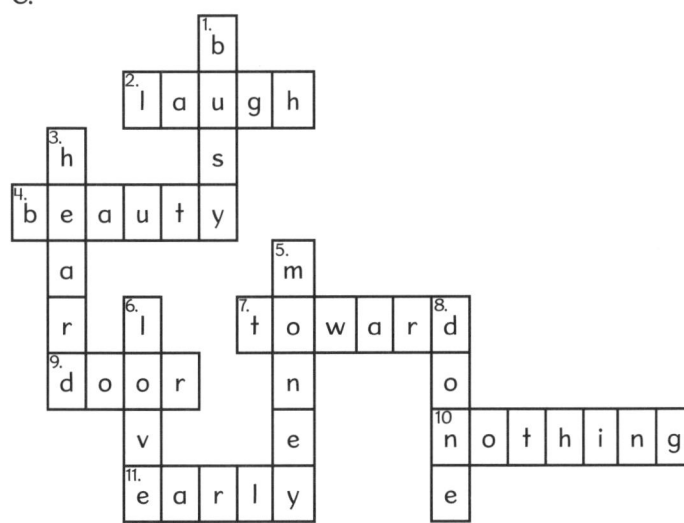

B. Answers can appear in any order within the column.

/shun/	/zhun/
fiction	illusion
emotion	submersion
mission	vision
condition	confusion

C. (bonus) enormous joyous (surplus)
   (artist) shortest weakest (orthodontist)
   (fungus) tallest obvious (cyclist)
   (circus) (dentist) fattest famous

D.
1. tall<u>est</u>
2. fam<u>ous</u>
3. dent<u>ist</u>
4. nerv<u>ous</u>
5. biolog<u>ist</u>
6. camp<u>us</u>
7. surp<u>lus</u>
8. smart<u>est</u>

Lesson 58: Other Suffixes (pp. 163-166)

Decoding

A. adoption caption detention
   explosion fiction isolation
   vacation reflection
   fam<u>ous</u> art<u>ist</u> cact<u>us</u>
   short<u>est</u>

Application Activities

A. Answers will vary
1. the explosion
2. emotions
3. an amputation
4. minor abrasions
5. famous

Lesson 59: Adding Suffixes to Words Ending in Y (pp. 167-168)

Decoding

A. brave bravely   happy happiest
   dry   dries   cloud cloudy
   slow   slowly   pony   ponies

Application Activities

A.
1. slow
2. cry
3. brave
4. gloom
5. glad
6. muliply

B.
1. happiest
2. playing
3. bravely
4. cloudy
5. keys

Answer Key

C. (grayest) ~~dryest~~ (trying) ~~ladyes~~ (windy)
~~strayes~~ ~~happyer~~ (rainy) (keys) ~~multiplyed~~

Great work!

Lesson 60: Practicing Multi-Syllabic Words (pp. 169-170)

Decoding

A.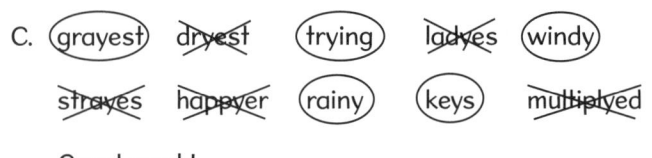

Application Activities

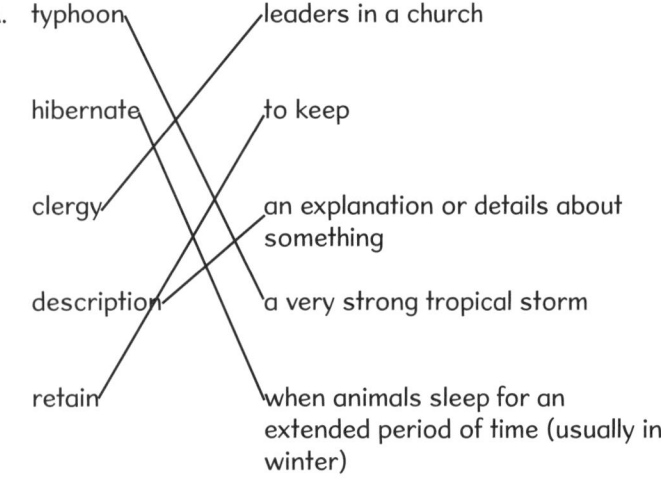

B.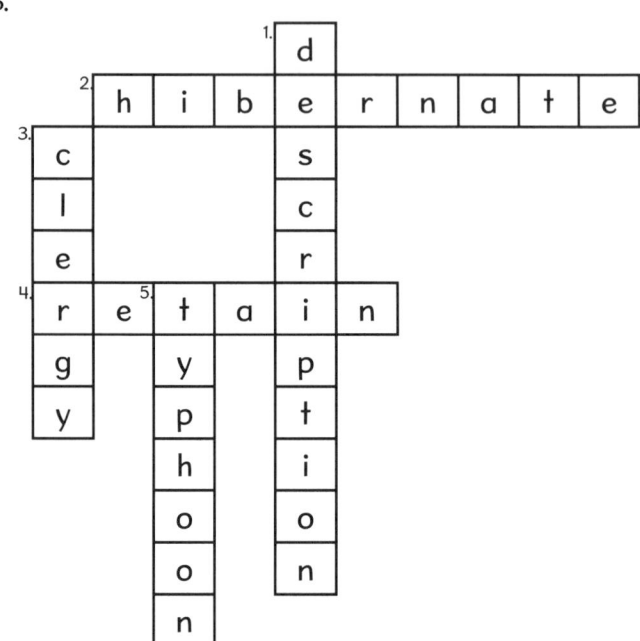

Lesson 61: Decoding Exceptions (pp. 173-174)

Decoding

A. river seven solid punish exam
finish study exist credit copy

Application Activities

A. 1. shadow, cabin
2. frigid
3. shiver
4. habit, visit, cabin, novel
5. magic

B.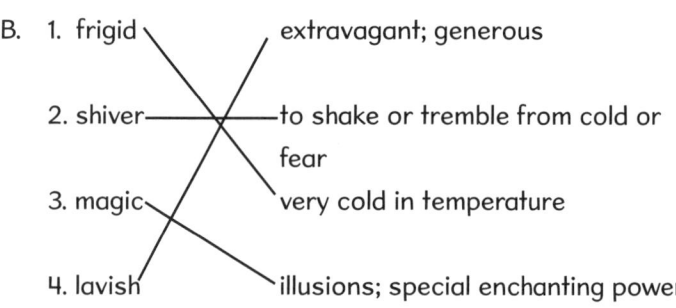

C. 1. lemon 4. dragon
2. credit 5. visit
3. solid

Student Workbook
Answer Key

D. 1. ă 6. ĕ
    2. ā 7. ē
    3. ă 8. ĕ
    4. ə 9. ī
    5. ē 10. ĭ

Lesson 62: Double Consonants and -KE, -CK, -K, and -C (pp. 175-176)

Decoding

A. acclaim   happy   hike   accent
   stuck   frantic   spark   traffic

Application Activities

A. Answers can appear in any order within each column.

/k/	/ks/
accomplish	accede
account	accept
accomodate	accident
acclaim	access

B. 1. hawk   6. take   11. duck
    2. oak   7. look   12. bark
    3. fork   8. speak 13. rock
    4. joke   9. trunk 14. music
    5. milk   10. panic 15. Pacific

Most Common Words List 13 (pp. 177-178)

A. My (brother) met a (woman) on the dance (floor) last week, and I (guess) he really likes her! In fact, he has a date with her tonight. He has (gone) to the store to (buy) new clothes, and he polished his (shoe) where he had a scuff mark. And now he wants to (lose) (weight)! He has never cared about doing these kinds of things for other (women) he's dated in the past. Maybe he's changed his point of (view) about needing to take better care of himself!

B. 1. floor   7. gone
    2. shoe   8. guess
    3. view   9. lose
    4. woman   10. buy
    5. brother 11. women
    6. weight

C. 1. (weightkrel); weight
    2. mlw(brother)h; brother
    3. (gone)skel; gone
    4. glin(buy); buy
    5. gt(floor)pe; floor
    6. vmep(view); view
    7. nas(lose); lose
    8. veks(guess); guess
    9. (shoe)meop; shoe
    10. fer(woman)b; woman
    11. kr(women)me; women

Lesson 63: Letter Combinations that Split (pp. 179-180)

Decoding

A. basket   discuss   cognate   disposal
   mister   history   gasket   ignore

Application Activities

A. 1. plastic
    2. history
    3. ignore

B. 1. ignore
    2. mister
    3. discuss

C. include   (mistake)   inflate   (disturb)
   express   (blister)   (system)   instrument
   (transpire)   (disposal)   represent   staple

Lesson 64: Spelling with -SS, -CE, or -SE (pp. 181-182)

Decoding

A. choice   class   fence   rice
   peace   spice   cheese   kiss

Answer Key

Application Activities

A. surprise, (nice), please, (ounce)
   cheese, (glass), (geese), (case)
   (trace), because, (fence), (prince)

B. 1. race
   2. pace
   3. class
   4. surpass
   5. course
   6. horse

C. 1. space, trace, lace — sp- tr- l- ~~sm-~~
   2. mice, twice, rice — m- tw- ~~fr-~~ r-
   3. dress, bless, press — dr- ~~ck-~~ bl- pr-
   4. blouse, mouse, spouse — bl- m- sp- ~~sh-~~

Lesson 65: Sounds of *EU* and *EW* (pp. 183-184)

Decoding

A. chew, sleuth, few, feud
   feudal, curfew, mildew, neutral

Application Activities

A. 1. sleuth
   2. renew
   3. pew
   4. eulogy
   5. feud

B. 1. sewer
   2. blew
   3. chew
   4. threw

C. stew

Lesson 66: Vowels that Reverse (pp. 185-186)

Decoding

A. video, aorta, diagram, medium
   dual, lion, trial, stadium

Application Activities

A. 1. ī
   2. ē
   3. ā
   4. ē
   5. ū
   6. ī

B. 1. ə
   2. ō
   3. ō
   4. ŭ
   5. ā
   6. ō

C. 1. rodeo
   2. stadium
   3. situate
   4. chaos

Lesson 67: Other Sounds of *EA* and *IE* (pp. 187-188)

Decoding

A. field, tie, rookie, vein, dream
   weigh, diet, bread, steak, perceive

Application Activities

A. Answers will vary.
   1. Margo's Steak Hosue
   2. health, wealth, weather
   3. tie
   4. his appetite
   5. eight

B. 1. veil — a cloth worn to cover the head
   2. thief — one who steals
   3. believe — to accept as true
   4. pleasant — enjoyable
   5. obedient — willing to follow a command

C. 1. ch; chief
   2. n; vein
   3. r; relieve

Lesson 68: Synonyms, Anotnyms, and More
    (pp. 189-190)

Application Activities

A. 1. amazing
   2. significant
   3. help
   4. funny

B. 1. soft   4. short
   2. wrong *or* left   5. strong
   3. hot   6. low

C. (fair/fair)   not/knot   [read/read]
   lone/loan   (quail/quail)   alter/altar
   [bow/bow]   cellar/seller   be/bee

D. 1. (radar)   4. (mom)
   2. (civic)   5. pets
   3. pool   6. (deed)

Glossary

adjacent vowel: two vowels standing together. Usually the second vowel is silent, and the first vowel is long. Exceptions are taught.

antonym: words that are the exact opposite

arc: (⌣) drawn under **Blends** and **Digraphs** to hold the consonants together and indicate they stay together

Blend: two or three consonants standing together, each letter keeping its own sound. Blends are marked with an **arc**.

bridge j: a connecting arc above *ge*, *gi*, and *gy* combinations. The letter *j* is placed over combinations to indicate that *g* says the sound of *j*.

bridge s: a connecting arc above *ce*, *ci*, and *cy* combinations. The letter *s* is placed over combinations to indicate *c* says the sound of *s*.

Decoding Skills: two skills that allow students to decode multi-syllabic words

Digraph: two consonants that stand together and make only one sound. Digraphs are marked with an **arc**.

Digraph Blend: a **Digraph** standing with *l*, *r*, or *s*. Both the Digraph and the added consonant are sounded.

Five Phonetic Skills: five skills that help students determine if the vowel sound will be short or long in a word

guardian consonant: one or two consonants following a vowel, causing the vowel to say its short sound

guardian star (*): a six-pointed star drawn above a **guardian consonant** to indicate the vowel sound will be short

heteronym: a word that is spelled the same as another but has a different meaning and sometimes a different pronunciation

homonym: a word that has the same sound (pronunciation) as another and usually the same spelling but a different meaning

homophone: a word that has the same sound (pronunciation) as another, but a different spelling and meaning

long vowel: when the vowel says its name

Glossary

mark: to identify with a symbol the sounds, including the vowel sound, within a word

Most Common Words (MCWs): high-frequency and sight words memorized to aid students in the reading process.

Murmur Diphthong: any of the five main vowels followed by the letter *r*, making a new vowel sound. Also known as *r*-controlled vowels, Murmur Diphthongs are marked with an *x* under the vowel and an **arc** under both letters.

palindrome: a word, verse, or sentence that reads the same forward and backward

prove: to identify with a symbol the sounds, including the vowel sound, within a word

schwa: an unstressed vowel sound represented by a symbol that resembles an upside-down *e* (ə). The schwa makes the sound of short *u*: /u/, as in *up*. All vowels can make the schwa sound.

short vowel: when the vowel says its sound

silent *e*: an *e* at the end of a word that is not sounded and makes the first vowel long

slide: one, two, or three initial consonants followed by a vowel. The sounds of the letters in a slide are blended, rather than separated. A slide is marked with a **slide arrow**. Sliding builds fluency.

slide arrow (→): an arrow drawn left to right under a **slide** to indicate the sounds in the slide are blended together

Special Vowel Combination: a three-letter combination containing a vowel followed by two consonants. The vowel sound is usually altered by the two following consonants.

Special Vowel Sound: vowel diphthong. It appears to be an **adjacent vowel** construction but does not follow the **adjacent vowel** rule; instead, it produces a new vowel sound. Special Vowel Sounds are marked with an *x* under and between both letters and an arc underneath.

synonym: a word that has the same meaning or nearly the same meaning as another word

voiced (⌣): This icon represents a **voiced** consonant. A **voiced** consonant is produced when the vocal cords are vibrating. Place your fingers on your throat over the vocal cords. Make a humming sound. You can feel your vocal cords vibrate as you say "mmmmm." All vowels are also voiced.

voiceless (⊖): This icon represents a **voiceless** consonant. A **voiceless** consonant produces no vibration of the vocal cords. Place your fingers on your throat over your vocal cords, and make the hissing sound "ssssssssss." You will not feel any vibration.